Spread Your Wings

And SOAR

Be transformed on the Winds of the Holy Spirit!

George Williams, Jr.

DEDICATION

To my Dad, a one-of-a-kind eagle. I would like to dedicate my first book to my father, Deacon George D. Williams Sr. It was because of his strong, focused, and diligent walk with our Lord Jesus Christ that I consider him a one-of-a-kind person with the Biblical characteristics of an eagle.

Deacon Williams, was a true example of a man that exhibited tenacity to stay in whatever fight he was needing to win. When it came to soul-winning, Deacon Williams would work tirelessly to win the hearts and minds of those within his circle of influence. Whether it was in his Christ Temple Sunday school class or whether it was on the streets of Butler Tarkington neighborhood in Indianapolis, Indiana, he was never afraid to witness for Jesus: no matter who it was.

When I was a child, the only book that I would see him reading was the Bible. His love for the scriptures was evident in his witness to the lost. He would extract his message anywhere between Genesis and Revelation to get his point across.

My dad never excelled to the level of many of his contemporaries, but yet at the same time, he was able to influence some of the great

leaders of this century. Deacon Williams was credited with influencing many of the great pulpits such as Pastor John Carey of Pasadena California, Elder Charles Mosley of Christ Temple Indianapolis, Doctor Willie J. Duncan of Muskegon Bible Institute, and many other men and women that went on to do great works in the kingdom of God.

This man of God was known throughout the country as, "Sidewalk Bishop," and could be found often in extensive dialog with Christian leaders from around the world. Many of the attributes of the eagle could be found in this man of God. His foresight to see potential leaders and souls for Jesus was profound. He would often use his tagline, "Do you have full coverage?" He would then begin his witness of Christ. He could see, with eagle eyes, their need for a Savior, and was fearless when flying in his zone. Standing only about 5 ft. tall never caused him to run from the assignment that he believed God had given him.

Today, I am honored to dedicate this book to my dad. He was a true Christian man that exhibited the very essence of the eagle throughout his life. Deacon Williams is an example of what it means to be a one-of-a-kind person with the Biblical characteristics of an eagle; one that always seeks to emulate the glorious attributes of Christ.

ACKNOWLEDGMENTS

Spread Your Wings and Soar

First, I would like to give thanks to God for His untiring love that He gives to us no matter what situation we find ourselves in. It is truly exciting to produce my first major writing! With nearly 45 years of ministry involvement: it took a pandemic to birth this powerful writing. It was around 2017 that I came across an internet article written by Michael Bradley called, "Traits of the Eagle and How It Pertains To Our Christian Walk." I would, every now and then, look over the notes, then put them away. But during the pandemic, I began seeking the Lord about what I needed to teach the people under my care. It was then that I was reminded of Isaiah 40:28-31. I then began building lessons to help encourage people during the Covid-19 pandemic.

I would like to acknowledge several key persons that have been an influence in my life. The first being Bishop James E. Tyson, Pastor John Livingston Rolle, Dr. E.Z. Sanders Sr., Apostle Raymond J. Keith Jr. and Bishop J. Laverne Tyson all made an impact on my spiritual journey. But the greatest influence on my life was Bishop William L. Bonner. He was a great example of a dynamic leader. I met Bishop Bonner in 1980 and was immediately drawn to him. I was in awe of his ingenious building ability and anointing to teach and preach. His commitment to serving God was extraordinary! I consider him to be the epitome of what a spiritual eagle can achieve through their dedication to God.

I would like to salute my dear brother and man of God, Aaron Beach, for his persistence in helping me get to the finish line. His humble spirit and deep love for the Word of God has been helpful in bringing out the beauty of this study. Also, I would like to thank sister Pamela Lynn for her assistance in collecting and transferring my video and teaching notes for this project. Last but not least, Lady Sarion, for her encouragement in everything that I endeavor to do for the Lord Jesus Christ. She has a great eye for detail and is assisting with the design of my book cover.

COPYRIGHT & FAIR USE

Spread Your Wings and Soar

SPREAD YOUR WINGS AND SOAR

Copyright & Fair Use

Scripture quotations marked "KJV" are taken from the Holy Bible, King James Version (Public Domain).

Scripture quotations marked "MSG" or "The Message" are taken from The Message. Copyright 1993, 1994, 1995, 1996, 2000, 2001, 2002. Used by permission of NavPress Publishing Group. http://www.navpress.com/

Scripture quotations marked "NKJV" are taken from the New King James Version. Copyright © 1982 by Thomas Nelson, Inc. Used by permission. All rights reserved. Bible text from the New King James Version® is not to be reproduced in copies or otherwise by any means except as permitted in writing by Thomas Nelson, Inc., Attn: Bible Rights and Permissions, P.O. Box 141000, Nashville, TN 37214-1000. http://www.nelsonbibles.com/

Bradley, Michael. "Traits of the Eagle and How It Pertains to Our Christian Walk" Bible Knowledge, (February 23, 2021), https://www.bible-knowledge.com/traits-of-eagle.

Images used by permission through Adobe Stock or were provided personally by the author.

TABLE OF CONTENTS

Spread Your Wings and Soar

SPREAD YOUR WINGS AND SOAR

Table of Contents

FOREWORD

Spread Your Wings and Soar

Dr. Waynette Samuel

There are some who are still reeling over the events of the past three years. So many are still searching for a space to call, "normal." This work by Bishop Williams is certainly a step in the right direction to re-establishing daily routines. This book is well worth reading and incorporating into our lives as a new, "normal."

During the last three years, much has changed; however, what has not changed and remains enduring, and unchangeable, is the Word of God. Bishop Williams addresses how God sees us and gives instructions on just how we can find our foundation again...by spreading our wings and soaring high! We are eagles; we can and must soar. While some are busy looking at the things around them, we must look higher; we must go higher. We are encouraged and compelled to go to a different level. A very important part of this book is its dependence upon the Word of God and how God sees us, His children, as eagles. Who can argue with that?

I am thankful for the release of this book because it encourages not only the unbeliever to begin to look towards God; but it also encourages the believer to seek higher ground in Christ through His Word. I encourage every reader of this book to first take out pen and paper, so that you can take notes as you read and incorporate the contents of this book into your everyday life. You are guaranteed to go higher as you read, ingest, digest, and utilize the information in this book.

Dr. Waynette Samuel
Next Level Nation Academy
Next Level Nation Ministries
Rahmah School of the Prophetic

Bishop Wendell C. Chinn

First of all, Bishop George Williams, Jr. is unashamedly Apostolic in Doctrine and Pentecostal in his Spiritual experience. His Christian roots are founded in the teaching he received from his family with his father, Deacon George Williams, Sr. laying the foundation for his son's ongoing Christian journey as husband, Pastor, and Bishop-Overseer. I consider it an honor to contribute to the foreward of his book, "Spread Your Wings and Soar."

Bishop Williams' interpretation of the revelations concerning the comparison of the Eagle and the Child of God is profound. His examples are also a representation of his own personal life as God's servant. Not to sound, "carnal," however, it appears God, "downloaded," His purpose and strategy for comparing the Eagle and the Child of God to Bishop Williams in a personal and special revelation.

As stated by Brother J. J. Pugh in his book, "The Battered Stake," "The Call of God adds strength and purpose to life." (p. 44). And this call is identical to why I feel Bishop Williams received his purpose in, "Spread Your Wings and Soar." This book will challenge the reader to allow God to capture their heart and desire to read his book and not to put it down until they finish. The reader will be encouraged as well as challenged to walk with God by word and deed as they soar with spiritual wings to the heights He has for the Believer. Lifestyles will change. Directions will change. Serious practical knowledge, wisdom, and understanding will be imparted as practical spiritual wisdom is imparted in its pages. Get ready to SPREAD YOUR WINGS AND SOAR. Amen.

Suffragan Bishop Wendell C. Chinn, MSW
Pastor, New Life Apostolic Church, Seymour Indiana
Co-Founder, Refining Fire Ministries International
Headquarters, Indianapolis, Indiana

Dr. Sunday J. Robert-Eze

I have known Bishop George Williams, Jr. for

over 20 years. In fact, not long after I arrived in the USA, and he has been a tremendous influence in my walk in the faith and ministry functions here in the US. He is indeed a father, an uncle, a brother, and a true helper. However, much more than the above, he is a true humble Christian servant leader who I will always want to hang out with anytime. He is a man of faith, prayer, and also much fun! He loves everyone, even those who do not follow Jesus. He loves the hip hop folks and the outcasts, and he loves many who don't even like him!

This is why I was delighted to be asked to write a foreword on his phenomenal book, "Spread your Wings and Soar." This book is definitely a MUST-READ for all Christians who want to understand the true walk with God.

In this book, Bishop George Williams, Jr. demonstrates his decades of walking with God. You will learn so many scriptures that will put you in a position to soar like an eagle. You will learn how to keep your faith so it doesn't fail. Bishop Williams has walked through real valleys and has come out shining for Jesus! This awesome book teaches a lot about how to pray an acceptable prayer to our Almighty God, which draws the difference between prayers that God will answer and the ones He won't answer.

The various characteristics of the eagle, which happens to be my favorite bird, was dissected and exposed by Bishop George in this piece, which will empower anyone to be as strong and powerful! I really can't wait for the rest of his books to get written and published. I therefore recommend this book to not just Christians but to anyone who wants to overcome any type of challenge in their life just like the eagle.

Sunday J Robert-Eze, Ph.D, FIC
Executive Director,
Missions Embassy Inc.

SPREAD YOUR WINGS AND SOAR

Foreword

CHAPTER 1

INTRODUCTION

THERE IS JUST SOMETHING ABOUT EAGLES

Have you ever looked outside and saw an eagle flying overhead? I am quite sure that you stopped what you were doing and watched until it left your view. There is something captivating and amazing about eagles! Personally, I have always admired eagles. In my office, you will find several pictures of eagles. The way they fly effortlessly, their beautiful plumage, and even their cry draws attention.

Watch how eagles soar through the air with their massive wings, then, take off after a fish they saw from a mile away: absolutely breathtaking!

Most eagles prefer to fly alone. They build their nests up high in the mountains and trees. Eagles do not back down from protecting their territory. They are honored and even worshiped among different cultures. They breed with one mate their entire lives. Eagles are patient and able to wait for long periods of time. They have eyes that are able to see 4-times better than a human. They build their nests in the wilderness, secluding themselves from others. Eagles also have distinguishing features that help us see them from a distance. There is just something about eagles!

YOU ARE GOD'S EAGLE 

Did you know that eagles are mentioned 26 times in scripture? I believe God wants to teach us something about the eagle; otherwise He would not have mentioned them this many times. What does God want to teach us?

As I studied scripture and researched the eagle, I found many similarities between an eagle and the life of a believer. Throughout this book you will see how the characteristics of the eagle relate to your walk with God. As you come to understand the eagle, I believe God will reveal who you are in Him. The characteristics of the eagle will take root in your life, and you will soar over every trial. God has a need of you; so, get ready to fly into your destiny!

> *Isaiah 40:28-31 MSG - God doesn't come and go. God lasts. He's Creator of all you can see or imagine. He doesn't get tired out, doesn't pause to catch His breath. And He knows everything, inside and out. He energizes those who get tired, gives fresh strength to dropouts. For even young people tire and drop out, young folk in their prime stumble and fall. But those who wait upon God get fresh strength. They spread their wings and soar like eagles. They run and don't get tired, they walk and don't lag behind.*

CHAPTER 2

LIVE ON HIGH GROUND

HIGH ABOVE

God has created the eagle to live on high ground. It is from this elevated position that they are able to spot their prey both on land and in water. They are known to build their large nests high in the mountains, away from everything. By doing this, it allows them to live with security and privacy.

The closest that I can identify with this height is when I visited the World Trade Center in New York City. I looked out from the observation deck and saw a spectacular view from that level. I can only imagine that the eagle living at that altitude experiences a peace that is unlike any other. As we look at the similarities of the eagle and the believer, it is clear that we must live on high ground.

> *Ephesians 2:6 NKJV - and raised [us] up together, and made [us] sit together in the heavenly [places] in Christ Jesus,*

THE ROCK THAT IS HIGHER THAN I

Psalms 61:2 in the amplified version expresses that the believer must seek to allow God to place us on a rock that is too high for us to reach without His help. As we live our lives in service to the Lord, we must live a life that depicts Christlikeness. Our walk, actions, lifestyle, and conversation should always be on a high level of righteous living unto God.

> *Psalms 61:2 AMP - From the end of the earth I call to You, when my heart is overwhelmed and weak; Lead me to the rock that is higher than I [a rock that is too high to reach without Your help].*

Apostle Paul lets us know that we are no longer to be conformed to the world, but are to be transformed by the renewing of our minds. The old creature that we were must be reborn into the image of our Lord Jesus Christ. By this, I mean that we must possess these godly attributes: holiness, righteousness, salvation from sin, and the process of sanctification.

> *Romans 12:1-2 AMP - 1 Therefore I urge you, brothers and sisters, by the mercies of God, to present your bodies [dedicating all of yourselves, set apart] as a living sacrifice, holy and well-pleasing to God, which is your rational (logical, intelligent) act of worship. 2 And do not be conformed to this world [any longer with its superficial values and customs], but be transformed and progressively changed [as you mature spiritually] by the renewing of your mind [focusing on godly values and ethical attitudes], so that you may prove [for yourselves] what the will of God is, that which is good and acceptable and perfect [in His plan and purpose for you].*

HOLINESS

Holiness is the act of holy living. The book of Leviticus gives us God's divine plan of holiness. God laid out how He wanted to be honored in worship and devotion to Him. He gave specific details on how the offerings and sacrifices were to be presented. Just as God had ordered how He wanted worship to be presented in the Old Testament, likewise in the New Testament, He desires for every believer to walk in holiness.

SPREAD YOUR WINGS AND SOAR

> *1 Peter 1:16 NKJV - because it is written, "Be holy, for I am holy."*

We are living in a society that does not hold holiness with great value.

Our world is motivated by humanism and the spirit of godlessness.

It is not hard to find Christians on low ground. Many believers do not want to walk in holiness. They want to make excuses why they keep falling; they fail to see that Christ came so that we could live on high ground.

1 Peter 2:9 says that God has called us out of darkness into a marvelous life. Because of this deliverance, we should habitually live on high ground. Even in a world that is full of corruption, sin, and ungodliness, we must pattern ourselves like the eagle, and dwell above the spirit of this age.

> *1 Chronicles 16:29 KJV - Give unto the LORD the glory due unto His name: bring an offering, and come before Him: worship the LORD in the beauty of holiness.*

Holiness must be a lifestyle that we seek to excel at as we live in service to the Lord 24/7.

SPREAD YOUR WINGS AND SOAR

Isaiah 35:8 NKJV - A highway shall be there, and a road, And it shall be called the Highway of Holiness. The unclean shall not pass over it, But it [shall be] for others. Whoever walks the road, although a fool, Shall not go astray.

The prophet Isaiah declared that holiness was a highway. This highway has very few travelers on it today, because so many in Christendom do not value living on high ground and choose to live like the present world.

Romans 6:19 ESV - I am speaking in human terms, because of your natural limitations. For just as you once presented your members as slaves to impurity and to lawlessness leading to more lawlessness, so now present your members as slaves to righteousness leading to sanctification.

As we live our lives unto the Lord, we must continually move away from allowing old habits to have control.

We must, in turn, surrender our bodies as holy servants unto Jesus. We can then live on high ground as we allow Christ to have His way in us.

SPREAD YOUR WINGS AND SOAR

> *2 Corinthians 7:1 ESV - Since we have these promises, beloved, let us cleanse ourselves from every defilement of body[fn] and spirit, bringing holiness to completion in the fear of God.*

As eagles, we must continue to purge ourselves from anything that will keep us from soaring in God. Everything that Satan tries to attach to our flesh and spirit will keep us from God's holiness. We want to remain holy by asking the Lord to search our hearts for any iniquity and letting Him cleanse us with the renewal of His Word.

> *Ephesians 4:23-24 NKJV - 23 and be renewed in the spirit of your mind, 24 and that you put on the new man which was created according to God, in true righteousness and holiness.*

Living on high ground allows us to become new in Christ Jesus. As we are renewed in the spirit, God's righteousness is created in us. Our new man is able to live holy because it operates by the spirit of God.

> *1 Thessalonians 3:13 NKJV - so that He may establish your hearts blameless in holiness before our God and Father at the coming of our Lord Jesus Christ with all His saints.*

Our divine design is to be established in holiness as saints of our Lord. We need to be rapture-ready when the trump is sounded.

1 Thessalonians 4:17 KJV - Then we which are alive and remain shall be caught up together with them in the clouds, to meet the Lord in the air: and so shall we ever be with the Lord.

Every blood-bought believer is looking forward to the day that we will be on high ground forever. We will share in the promise of our Savior that He will return and meet us in the air. What a glorious day!

RIGHTEOUSNESS

We have to realize that righteousness cannot be obtained on our own. No amount of religious effort, discipline, law-keeping, or self-improvement can make us right with God.

We can only receive right-standing with God through Christ Jesus.

Praise God that He exchanges our sins and shortcomings with His complete righteousness! To know Christ and to make Him known should be our goal, and it is up to us to keep our relationship with

Jesus as our first priority. Until the day He calls us home or returns, we should want to be found on high ground in Him!

> *Psalm 145:17 KJV - The Lord is righteous in all His ways, and holy in all His works.*
>
> *Philippians 3:9 ESV - and be found in Him, not having a righteousness of my own that comes from the law, but that which comes through faith in Christ, the righteousness from God that depends on faith—*

We have right standing in Him because we are covered by His righteous blood that He shed on Calvary for us. Christ died for us, so the least we can do is live for Him! Glory to God, for we are the righteousness of God through Christ Jesus!

> *2 Corinthians 5:21 KJV - For He hath made Him [to be] sin for us, who knew no sin; that we might be made the righteousness of God in Him.*

SALVATION

Salvation can be defined as being delivered from sin. This is the reason Christ came into the world; to set at liberty those that were captured by the grip of sin. When we look at the eagle, we see a bird that is totally free. That is the intention of our Savior: that we can live a life that is free from the bondage of Satan's grip. That is why it is so important for believers to understand that church membership is not salvation! To have one's name on a church roll does not secure one's soul from eternal damnation. It may be popular to be associated with a church or ministry that appears to have the acceptance of the masses; but in reality, it is no more than a social organization.

Being on high ground means that one desires to be free from the slavery of sin.

John 3:17 CEV - God did not send His Son into the world to condemn its people. He sent Him to save them!

There was no need to condemn the world because those that live in sin know that they are living ungodly.

Acts 4:12 NKJV - Nor is there salvation in any other, for there is no other name under heaven given among men by which we must be saved.

Nothing is able to save us except the name of Jesus. There is no other means for us to receive deliverance from the power, pollution, and penalty that sin brings to mankind.

> *Psalms 27:1 KJV - A Psalm of David. The LORD is My Light and My Salvation; whom shall I fear? the LORD is the Strength of My Life; of whom shall I be afraid?*

Deliverance is what frees the believer from the snare of Satan. We get our strength from the Lord, who is the Light that lightens our path as we soar doing the work of the ministry.

> *Psalms 62:2 KJV - He only is my rock and my salvation; He is my defense; I shall not be greatly moved.*

As God's eagle, we will not be intimidated by Satan's threats against us.

We can rest assured that our God is a defense, and we cannot be moved from our place in God.

> *Isaiah 12:2 KJV - Behold, God is My Salvation; I will trust, and not be afraid: for the LORD JEHOVAH is My Strength and My Song; He also is become My Salvation.*

The prophet Isaiah joyfully states that his God was his salvation. This should be the declaration of all the people of God: to know assuredly where our salvation in Christ is, and to know that in Him only can we trust. Our trust and faith cannot be in church membership, but in the deliverance that we received from Christ at Calvary.

> *Isaiah 12:3 NKJV - Therefore with joy you will draw water from the wells of salvation.*

The wells of salvation flow freely, and are available for whosoever desires to draw from this well. There is an unspeakable joy to those that want to receive this gift of eternal life.

SANCTIFICATION

Believers should be living set apart.

> **Every believer should allow the Holy Spirit to do His work of sanctification in their lives.**

God has called us to be different. He has equipped us through the Holy Spirit to operate in the power of His Spirit. We cannot allow ourselves to be lowered to the level of those who have an immature understanding of who they are in God. Because God has called us to be eagles, we cannot lower ourselves to become chickens that have no ability to operate as an eagle!

To be sanctified means that we exhibit a spiritual change that has taken place because of the transforming power of God. We have been changed because God has done His redemptive work in our lives. He has changed us because He has a specific work that He wants to do through us. That is why He has allowed us to be set apart for His use.

> When we have been set apart, we are no longer focused on a lower mindset, but seek to soar as an eagle.

1 Corinthians 1:30 AMP - But it is from Him that you are in Christ Jesus, who became to us wisdom from God [revealing His plan of salvation], and righteousness [making us acceptable to God], and sanctification [making us holy and setting us apart for God], and redemption [providing our ransom from the penalty for sin],

> Right living must be the focus and desire of every born-again believer.

Seeking to walk in righteousness is the most important attribute that we should desire. To do what is right in the sight of God, should be our aim as we soar on the Holy Spirit as our Guide. Our lives must exhibit the example of one that is seeking to please our Lord by doing His will.

> *2 Thessalonians 2:13 ESV - But we ought always to give thanks to God for you, brothers beloved by the Lord, because God chose you as the firstfruits to be saved, through sanctification by the Spirit and belief in the truth.*

SUMMARY

In summary, eagles nest high in the mountains, which gives them a grand view. Not many things will bother an eagle since they are so high up. For the believer this means that we should live in holiness, righteousness, receive salvation from sin, and allow the process of sanctification to take place if we are to showcase the power of God through our lives. We are to be living on a different level than the world. We are not chickens that are doomed to the ground; no, we are mighty eagles that have set themselves on high ground. Through the power of the Holy Spirit you are able to nest in heavenly heights, you righteous eagle.

PRAYER

Father, in the mighty name of Jesus, we thank You for allowing us to desire to stay on high ground.

As we continue to grow and mature in You as our Lord and Savior, please teach us to seek after Your holiness, to walk in Your righteousness, to allow the Holy Spirit to sanctify us, and make us what You have designed our lives to be through Your divine plan. Help us to always value the great plan of salvation that You purchased with Your own blood. Father God, I pray that this reader will be impacted through Your Holy Spirit to always want to dwell on high ground as You have instinctively put in the eagle. In Jesus' name. Amen.

CHAPTER 3

SKILLED FLIERS

EAGLES LEARN TO SOAR

Eagles are skilled fliers. They can fly up to an altitude of 15,000 feet; when they are that high, they do not flap their wings, but instead, they glide through the air. Eagles are born with large wings; a typical wingspan is about seven feet. These wings require much energy to move. However, the eagle's wings were not created to be flapped: they were created to soar. If they were to flap though, they would waste all their energy and plummet to the ground: dying in the process.

Eagles learn to observe wind thermals and glide on the currents; this is the secret to their gliding. They can wait for days until a strong wind thermal is able to take them where they need to go. Just like eagles, we also fly on wings and wind thermals. Our left wing is our faith in God. Our right wing is our belief in God.

The Holy Spirit is the wind thermal that carries us.

Zechariah 4:6 KJV - ...Not by might, nor by power, but by My Spirit, saith the Lord of Hosts.

Eagles must spread out their wings and trust that the wind thermals will carry them. We must spread out our wings of faith and belief in God to allow the Holy Spirit to carry us.

We cannot lean on our own understanding.

We are soaring on the Holy Spirit. We have confidence that the Spirit of God undergirds us.

Proverbs 3:5-6 MSG - "Trust God from the bottom of your heart; don't try to figure out everything on your own. Listen for God's voice in everything you do, everywhere you go; He's the one who will keep you on track. Don't assume that you know it all."

God sustains and keeps us, and just like the eagle, there are times when we must wait for the wind to blow just right. We have to learn to fly on the Holy Spirit. We cannot do anything without His anointing. Anointing can be defined as God's power: operating through us to do whatever He needs. He will give us the what, when, and how: just trust Him!

Psalms 27:14 KJV - "Wait on the LORD: be of good courage, and He shall strengthen thine heart: wait, I say, on the LORD."

FAITH, BELIEF, AND THE HOLY SPIRIT

There are three main points about faith, belief, and the Holy Spirit I would like to bring out. If you can understand these truths, you will soar through life just like the eagle. Be expecting to receive from the Lord as you take flight and read these following truths!

1: BE LED BY THE HOLY SPIRIT

Be dependent on Him. Listen for His voice. Trust that the Holy Spirit is more than enough. Trust He will not let you down.

SPREAD YOUR WINGS AND SOAR

**Read His Word so you
can line up your thoughts with His.**

*Romans 12:2 NKJV - And do not be conformed to
this world, but be transformed by the renewing
of your mind, that you may prove what [is] that
good and acceptable and perfect will of God.*

Let us look at the life of Elijah. He moved
mightily in miracles through the power of the Holy
Spirit. He was doing great until Jezebel threatened
his life and frightened him. He ran far away, and
asked the Lord to take His life; for he thought he was
the only believer alive. Read below and see how God
dealt with him.

*1 Kings 19:11-13 NKJV - 11 Then He said, "Go
out, and stand on the mountain before the
LORD." And behold, the LORD passed by, and a
great and strong wind tore into the mountains
and broke the rocks in pieces before the LORD,
[but] the LORD [was] not in the wind; and after
the wind an earthquake, [but] the LORD [was] not
in the earthquake; 12 and after the earthquake
a fire, [but] the LORD [was] not in the fire; and
after the fire a still small voice. 13 So it was, when
Elijah heard [it], that he wrapped his face in his
mantle and went out and stood in the entrance
of the cave. Suddenly a voice [came] to him, and
said, "What are you doing here, Elijah?"*

Elijah got all bent out of shape due to Jezebel's intimidation. God knew that Elijah needed to be elsewhere. He knew that Elijah was running away for his life. What did God do? He told him to stand outside the cave. Elijah saw a great windstorm tear apart a mountain, but God was not in that. He felt a strong tremor, but God was not in that. He saw a wildfire appear, but God was not in that either. It was with the still small voice that God revealed Himself to Elijah.

> **Many distractions will try to take your focus away from hearing the voice of God.**

Can you imagine how loud a windstorm of that caliber would be? How about an earthquake? Even fires have a sound. These were not quiet events! Yet, God spoke in a still (peaceful) small (quiet) voice. Being led by the Holy Spirit will require your focus. You must know what His voice sounds like even when all these loud things come against you. Know that God wants to speak into your situations; you are able to hear His voice because You are His precious sheep.

> *John 10:3-5 CEV - 2-3 But the gatekeeper opens the gate for the shepherd, and he goes in through it. The sheep know their shepherd's voice. He*

> *calls each of them by name and leads them out. 4 When he has led out all of his sheep, he walks in front of them, and they follow, because they know his voice. 5 The sheep will not follow strangers. They don't recognize a stranger's voice, and they run away.*

⧓ **You have to know what His Word says.** ⧓

Jesus Christ, Himself, used the Word to rebuke Satan. Since Jesus, the Living Word of God, needed the written Word, then how much more do we!?

> *Matthew 4:4 KJV - But He answered and said, It is written, Man shall not live by bread alone, but by every word that proceedeth out of the mouth of God.*

The Word is your daily bread. Feed your spirit with food that only comes from God. Do not starve yourself or you will not have enough energy to lift your wings. Treat His Word like you would a meal. Do you skip breakfast, lunch, or dinner? No! Then do not skip out on your spiritual food. You need the energy, encouragement, exhortation, and revelation He supplies to you!

⧓ **The more you get into His Word; the more you will recognize His voice.** ⧓

The more you recognize His voice; the more you can follow His direction. The more you follow His direction; the better your life will be. Choose to read His Word, and you will make it easier to be led by the Holy Spirit.

2: WALK IN THE ANOINTING

There is a special calling on your life; no one else has the same calling as you. There is a specific place He has assigned to you, but you have to use your wings to get there! You must have confidence that He will uphold you. It is time for you to jump off the cliff, and soar on the Holy Spirit!

Galatians 5:25 KJV - *"If we live in the Spirit, let us also walk in the Spirit."*

Let us look at the life of Moses. He was a Hebrew child adopted by the daughter of Pharaoh. He grew up with the best instruction, and all his needs were taken care of. However, Moses did things differently. He did not identify with the Egyptians. He could not ignore the plight of his Hebrew brothers and sisters. He thought he was able to take matters into his own hands. He sensed the call of God on his life, but he got hasty and made a bad decision. He saw a brother being treated wrongly and killed the oppressor. He thought it was hidden, but everyone knew. He was forced to run away from everything, and eventually, ended up in the desert town of Midian, where he learned to tend sheep. However, the gifts and callings of God are without repentance; God did not forget Moses' purpose.

Romans 11:29 KJV - For the gifts and calling of God are without repentance.

Moses needed to learn how to walk in his anointing. He knew there was something special about himself, but he did not know how to walk it out. So, God in His infinite wisdom, stowed Moses away in Midian to learn humility. Midian, at that time, was a peaceful and quiet environment where he could learn to follow God. When the time came for Moses to walk into the next phase of his life: that is when God appeared to him. Many of us recognize we have a calling placed on our lives, and we can even see the calling on others' lives as well. However, we must fully rely on God's guidance to help us walk in our anointing; for our own striving will never lead us to where He needs us.

Exodus 3:2-4 NKJV - 2 And the Angel of the Lord appeared to him in a flame of fire from the

> *midst of a bush. So he looked, and behold, the bush was burning with fire, but the bush was not consumed. 3 Then Moses said, "I will now turn aside and see this great sight, why the bush does not burn." 4 So when the Lord saw that he turned aside to look, God called to him from the midst of the bush and said, "Moses, Moses!" And he said, "Here I am."*

Like a flaming bush, God appeared to Moses. Now, Moses had a choice here. He could have walked away. He could have ignored this amazing sight. He could have been caught up in his daily chores and let time dictate his actions, but no, he turned to see what this was about. When God saw that Moses was ready and willing: He then talked with him. When God sees your heart as ready and willing, then He can guide you to the next place.

**Be open to instruction
from the Holy Spirit!**

Now, let us skip down to the next point of our story.

> *Exodus 4:1-4 KJV - 1 Then Moses answered and said, "But suppose they will not believe me or listen to my voice; suppose they say, 'The Lord has not appeared to you.' " 2 So the Lord said to him, "What is that in your hand?" He said, "A rod." 3 And He said, "Cast it on the ground."*

SPREAD YOUR WINGS AND SOAR

> *So he cast it on the ground, and it became a serpent; and Moses fled from it. 4 Then the Lord said to Moses, "Reach out your hand and take it by the tail" (and he reached out his hand and caught it, and it became a rod in his hand),*

Moses goes through a laundry list of excuses for why he does not want to be the mouthpiece of God. God is not having it and asks Moses a question. "What is that in your hand?" God is not blind. He knew exactly what it was. He wanted to hear it from Moses himself. All of the shepherding that Moses had done was preparation to be the shepherd for the Israelites; but he did not know that. He had no clue that the rod he used for herding sheep would be the same rod that would split the Red Sea. He thought he had run away from his destiny. I wonder if Moses had dreams about the murder of that Egyptian? Did he wonder if he would ever fulfill God's plan in his life? Did he dream about his brothers and sisters being tortured by their taskmasters? If he had no compassion, then I do not believe God would have come back for him. Moses had an intense desire to fulfill his calling. He could not run away from his destiny because it was rooted in him.

Many of us have thought we ran away from God. That God cannot use me because of such and such. That I have no special talents, or that I cannot do something as well as such and such. We come up with all the excuses, and yet all God is asking is, "What is in your hand?" What is it that you have a talent for? What is it that you are gifted in?

> He has given you a special anointing to do things no one else can.

You are uniquely created to make an impact for God. We all have something that God wants us to do. How can you serve God to the best of your ability? Ask yourself that question, and let God reveal the answer to your heart.

God wants you to know that He has a need of your talents. He put them in you for such a time as this.

> God knows what He is doing!

Trust Him to help you figure out your place. Ask Him to strengthen what you have. Surrender your talents to Him. You see, Moses threw his rod on the ground at the request of the Lord. That was an act of surrender. Moses could have said no; but He wanted to please God. Throw your talents on the ground before the Lord, and watch as He uses them mightily for His Kingdom purpose. God will help you walk out the anointing in your life. Trust Him!

3: HAVE CONFIDENCE IN GOD

You must have faith and belief in God. Otherwise, you will not accomplish God's will or plan for your life. You cannot be afraid or fearful. He has equipped you for such a time as this. If the eagle does not leave their perch, they will die of starvation.

Those who have no courage in God shall accomplish nothing.

Without faith… you cannot soar. Without belief… you cannot glide. You must have both. Your faith is your conviction in God. Your belief is your trust in Him. You must be fully convinced that God is who He says He is, and then, you must trust in Him. You will then allow yourself to soar through life with confidence.

Hebrews 11:6 CEV - But without faith no one can please God. We must believe that God is real and rewards everyone who searches for Him.

We are going to read from the book of Daniel. Shadrach, Meshach and Abednego were in a dilemma. They either had to worship the statue made by King Nebuchadnezzar, or perish in a fiery furnace.

SPREAD YOUR WINGS AND SOAR

Skilled Fliers | Chapter 3

> *Daniel 3:4-6 NKJV - 4 Then a herald cried [a] aloud: "To you it is commanded, O peoples, nations, and languages, 5 that at the time you hear the sound of the horn, flute, harp, lyre, and psaltery, in symphony with all kinds of music, you shall fall down and worship the gold image that King Nebuchadnezzar has set up; 6 and whoever does not fall down and worship shall be cast immediately into the midst of a burning fiery furnace."*

These Hebrew men decided to follow their God. They knew that He would not be pleased if they worshiped another. They stuck to their convictions and trusted in God.

The Chaldeans were watching them and saw that they did not bow and worship the statue. They brought accusations against them. You must know that people are watching you.

**Live your life to be pleasing
in the sight of the Lord.**

Do not cause others to stumble based on your actions. These Hebrew men were not about to corrupt themselves by worshiping another god. Read below to see how the story unfolds.

SPREAD YOUR WINGS AND SOAR

Daniel 3:12-15 NKJV - 12 There are certain Jews whom you have set over the affairs of the province of Babylon: Shadrach, Meshach, and Abed-Nego; these men, O king, have not paid due regard to you. They do not serve your gods or worship the gold image which you have set up." 13 Then Nebuchadnezzar, in rage and fury, gave the command to bring Shadrach, Meshach, and Abed-Nego. So they brought these men before the king. 14 Nebuchadnezzar spoke, saying to them, "Is it true, Shadrach, Meshach, and Abed-Nego, that you do not serve my gods or worship the gold image which I have set up? 15 Now if you are ready at the time you hear the sound of the horn, flute, harp, lyre, and psaltery, in symphony with all kinds of music, and you fall down and worship the image which I have made, good! But if you do not worship, you shall be cast immediately into the midst of a burning fiery furnace. And who is the god who will deliver you from my hands?"

They are given one last chance. Worship the golden statue or die in a fiery furnace. Talk about pressure! This is a serious situation. Satan is really intensifying the stakes.

When it looks like there is no way out... but God!

He can make a way where there is no way. He can supersede our physical laws and do things only He can do. He is a miracle-working God; you can trust that He is watching over you. Believe in His goodness and watch deliverance unfold! Read their response below.

> *Daniel 3:16-18 NKJV - 16 Shadrach, Meshach, and Abed-Nego answered and said to the king, "O Nebuchadnezzar, we have no need to answer you in this matter. 17 If that is the case, our God whom we serve is able to deliver us from the burning fiery furnace, and He will deliver us from your hand, O king. 18 But if not, let it be known to you, O king, that we do not serve your gods, nor will we worship the gold image which you have set up."*

There it is! You can see their faith and belief in God in their statement. They believed that God could deliver them from the furnace. Now, there was no instance in history where God did something like this. It was not written for them to read. They were not alive at the time when God did miracles daily for the Israelites on their way to the promised land. They had no specific example they could point out, but what they did have… faith and belief. They knew their God was all-powerful. They had the faith to believe God for a miracle that had never happened before. They trusted God and they even said if He does not save us, know that we will not worship your gods or golden image. Such amazing faith! They were ready to die in the name of God. They would be martyrs and examples to others. Read below to see how the story ends.

Daniel 3:19-25 NKJV - 19 Then Nebuchadnezzar was full of fury, and the expression on his face changed toward Shadrach, Meshach, and Abed-Nego. He spoke and commanded that they heat the furnace seven times more than it was usually heated. 20 And he commanded certain mighty men of valor who were in his army to bind Shadrach, Meshach, and Abed-Nego, and cast them into the burning fiery furnace. 21 Then these men were bound in their coats, their trousers, their turbans, and their other garments, and were cast into the midst of the burning fiery furnace. 22 Therefore, because the king's command was urgent, and the furnace exceedingly hot, the flame of the fire killed those men who took up Shadrach, Meshach, and Abed-Nego. 23 And these three men, Shadrach, Meshach, and Abed-Nego, fell down bound into the midst of the burning fiery furnace. 24 Then King Nebuchadnezzar was astonished; and he rose in haste and spoke, saying to his [b] counselors, "Did we not cast three men bound into the midst of the fire?" They answered and said to the king, "True, O king." 25 "Look!" he answered, "I see four men loose, walking in the midst of the fire; and they are not hurt, and the form of the fourth is like the[c] Son of God."

Even in the midst of the fiery furnace they were never alone! Though a normal man in this situation would have died and even some of his own soldiers died… they were kept safe. They had great faith and belief in God to deliver them, and deliver them He did in grandiose fashion! There is a Fourth Man in the fire; His name is Jesus! He will never leave or forsake you for any reason. They did not know how God was going to deliver them, but believed that whatever the outcome was going to be was His will. Because they trusted in the God they served.

> **We might not always see how God wants to turn around a bad situation, but we know that He is able to do it; nothing is impossible for God.**

Have faith and belief that He wants you to fly far into the destiny He has prepared for your life.

Hebrews 13:5-6 AMPC - 5 Let your character or moral disposition be free from love of money [including greed, avarice, lust, and craving for earthly possessions] and be satisfied with your present [circumstances and with what you have]; for He [God] Himself has said, I will not in any way fail you nor give you up nor leave you without support. [I will] not, [I will] not, [I will] not in any degree leave you helpless nor forsake nor let [you] down (relax My hold on you)! [Assuredly not!] 6 So we take comfort and are encouraged and confidently and boldly say, The Lord is my Helper; I will not be seized with alarm [I will not fear or dread or be terrified]. What can man do to me?

SUMMARY

In summary, do not tire yourself out flapping trying to make something happen on your own. Do not stay perched on the cliff being unable to make a decision to jump because you do not know if you will survive. You were not born to fall or fail; you were designed to trust in the Lord. Rest in the promise of the Holy Spirit to lead you along in life. Walk in the anointing that God has given you. He is with you through it all. You can trust in Him. You have been appointed by God to soar as His eagle! Fly on with the Holy Spirit, you soaring eagle.

PRAYER

Father, I thank You for these precious readers and the opportunity to reach out and touch their hearts with Your Word. I ask for boldness and courage, for them to not stay perched on the cliff. Show them that they have all the qualities and traits of the eagle. Help us all to not be afraid to trust in You. We realize that our wings are our faith and belief in You. We cannot do anything without Your Spirit. We thank You for Your Spirit undergirding us and causing us to be able to soar. Whatever call that is on these readers' lives, I ask that You give them the courage to step up and do whatever it is You have assigned them to do. In the precious name of Jesus Christ I pray. Amen.

CHAPTER 4

MAJESTIC

ROYAL BIRDS

Eagles have a regal attribute about them. Due to their behavior and demeanor; eagles seem to be extraordinary. They rule over the air as kings of the sky. Likewise, we Christians have been born into royalty due to our adoption into God's family. Royal blood now runs through our veins. We are now kings and priests unto the Lord, all because of Jesus' sacrifice.

Revelation 1:5-6 CEV - 5 May kindness and peace be yours from Jesus Christ, the faithful witness. Jesus was the first to conquer death, and He is the ruler of all earthly kings. Christ loves us, and by His blood He sets us free from our sins. 6 He

SPREAD YOUR WINGS AND SOAR

lets us rule as kings and serve God His Father as priests. To Him be glory and power forever and ever! Amen.

Looking back at the Old Testament, we see God's heart was for all Israel to be priests unto Him. God was looking for a nation that would serve Him wholeheartedly. A people He could identify as His own possession.

Exodus 19:6 KJV – And ye shall be unto me a kingdom of priests, and a holy nation. These are the words which thou shalt speak unto the children of Israel.

This was a foreshadowing of things to come. Through the blood of Jesus Christ, we have been made a holy people unto God. Even Israel, God's chosen nation, was not truly holy.

Our right-standing in God does not come from any good works that we have done.

Only through the atoning blood of Jesus, are we able to be kings and priests before Him. Fleshly works cannot erase the stain of sin. Only Jesus, who fulfilled the law, was able to break sin's hold on us.

Romans 3:20-25 AMP - 20 For no person will be justified [freed of guilt and declared righteous] in His sight by [trying to do] the works of the Law. For through the Law we become conscious of sin [and the recognition of sin directs us toward repentance, but provides no remedy for sin]. 21 But now the righteousness of God has been clearly revealed [independently and completely] apart from the Law, though it is [actually] confirmed by the Law and the [words and writings of the] Prophets. 22 This righteousness of God comes through faith in Jesus Christ for all those [Jew or Gentile] who believe [and trust in Him and acknowledge Him as God's Son]. There is no distinction, 23 since all have sinned and continually fall short of the glory of God, 24 and are being justified [declared free of the guilt of sin, made acceptable to God, and granted eternal life] as a gift by His [precious, undeserved] grace, through the redemption [the payment for our sin] which is [provided] in Christ Jesus, 25 whom God displayed publicly [before the eyes of the world] as a [life-giving] [c]sacrifice of atonement and reconciliation (propitiation) by His blood [to be received] through faith. This was to demonstrate His righteousness [which demands punishment for sin], because in His forbearance [His deliberate restraint] He passed over the sins previously committed [before Jesus' crucifixion].

DUTIES OF THE PRIEST 

We see, though, that the Tabernacle in the Old Testament is a type and shadow of our service in the New Testament. Let us look at the duties of a priest. There are four main points I will bring out.

> *1 Peter 2:9-10 CEV - 9 But you are God's chosen and special people. You are a group of royal priests and a holy nation. God has brought you out of darkness into His marvelous light. Now you must tell all the wonderful things He has done. The Scriptures say, 10 "Once you were nobody. Now you are God's people. At one time no one had mercy on you. Now God has treated you with kindness."*

1: PRAYER

In American Indian tradition, the eagle is a messenger between the gods and the people. During the Sun Dance, the eagle is symbolized throughout with items such as whistles, feathers, and talons. They use a fan, often made of eagle feathers, to direct what they believe to be positive healing energy towards sick people. The fan is then held up, and it is believed that the eagles take the prayers for the sick to their gods. Using this example, even the world understands that prayer is a vital part of a priest's service.

Prayer is defined simply as communicating with God. In the Old Testament, priests were limited in their communication with God. They had to follow everything by the book of the Law. There was no room for doing things their way. They had to follow sacrificial practices to the letter. They could not enter into the presence of God: the Holy of Holies. They could not touch the Ark of the Covenant. They could not go beyond the veil. There was a clear separation between them and God. What a hard thing this must have been for them! They could still pray to God with their words; but they could not see the true character of God through all of the Law's regulations.

Through Jesus, we have been set free from the requirements of the Law! We are able to enter into His presence. We are able to touch His heart. He lives on the inside of us: His holy temples. We are able to have a deeper and closer relationship than they could in the Old Testament.

Colossians 3:16 NKJV - Let the word of Christ dwell in you richly in all wisdom, teaching and admonishing one another in psalms and hymns and spiritual songs, singing with grace in your hearts to the Lord.

It was said of David that he was a man after God's own heart. When we examine David's life, we can see the way into God's heart is through prayer and praise. Read the psalm below and see. There are plenty more examples of David choosing to pray, praise, and thank God no matter what the circumstances were.

> *Psalms 100:1-5 CEV - 1 Shout praises to the Lord, everyone on this earth. 2 Be joyful and sing as you come in to worship the Lord! 3 You know the Lord is God! He created us, and we belong to Him; we are His people, the sheep in His pasture. 4 Be thankful and praise the Lord as you enter His temple. 5 The Lord is good! His love and faithfulness will last forever.*

No matter what David went through he was able to give praise to the Lord. His life is a great example for us to follow. Paul also makes mention of these same concepts.

> *1 Thessalonians 5:16-18 CEV - 16 Always be joyful 17 and never stop praying. 18 Whatever happens, keep thanking God because of Jesus Christ. This is what God wants you to do.*

Paul is writing to the believers in Thessalonica: a heavily persecuted church body. What does he tell them? Always be joyful, never stop praying, and keep thanking God. Even if they take your freedoms away, even if they throw you in prison, and even if they attempt to kill you, stay joyful, pray, and thank God.

> **There is no excuse for the believer that should ever stop their joy, their prayer life, or their attitude of thanksgiving.**

Paul again makes mention of these same truths to the Philippians… while he was in prison! If we could get a grasp of this, our lives would be so much better!

> *Philippians 4:4-7 AMP - 4 Rejoice in the Lord always [delight, take pleasure in Him]; again I will say, rejoice! 5 Let your gentle spirit [your graciousness, unselfishness, mercy, tolerance, and patience] be known to all people. The Lord is near. 6 Do not be anxious or worried about anything, but in everything [every circumstance and situation] by prayer and petition with thanksgiving, continue to make your [specific] requests known to God. 7 And the peace of God [that peace which reassures the heart, that peace] which transcends all understanding, [that peace which] stands guard over your hearts and your minds in Christ Jesus [is yours].*

There is nothing that should get us so bent out of shape that we cannot pray and thank God. No if's, and's, or but's about it; as a priest of the Most High God, you will find it is a joy and privilege to pray and thank God in the midst of the trial, because you know it is going to turn around in your favor. Jesus also talked about prayer. Let us read what He said.

> *Luke 18:1 AMP - Now Jesus was telling the disciples a parable to make the point that at all times they ought to pray and not give up and lose heart,*

Jesus is encouraging us to keep praying! As our Example of the Faith, Jesus is constantly interceding on our behalf! He is covering us with His grace continually.

> *Romans 8:34 CEV - Or can anyone condemn them? No indeed! Christ died and was raised to life, and now He is at God's right side, speaking to Him for us.*

Do not faint, lose heart, or give up.

Prayer is not begging God, but it is affirming what God has said and standing on it with full faith.

You have to understand this; prayer should be more about thanking God for who He is than complaining about situations in your life.

> *Luke 21:36 CEV - Watch out and keep praying that you can escape all that is going to happen and that the Son of Man will be pleased with you.*

Keep praying that your way may be established in truth. Prayer sets up your pathway. You can make your day easier to handle by praying and thanking God. Jesus was found praying often. Paul the Apostle firmly believed in consistent prayer.

> *2 Thessalonians 1:11-12 NKJV - 11 Therefore we also pray always for you that our God would count you worthy of [this] calling, and fulfill all the good pleasure of [His] goodness and the work of faith with power, 12 that the name of our Lord Jesus Christ may be glorified in you, and you in Him, according to the grace of our God and the Lord Jesus Christ.*

Paul is asking that you would be worthy of the calling God has chosen you for. You are called to pray and give thanks! It is a majestic thing when you can watch God work through your prayer and thanksgiving to bring forth a miracle!

2: SACRIFICE

The next duty of the priesthood is to offer sacrifices. Only a trained priest would understand the ins-and-outs of the sacrificial practices. Let us look at which New Testament sacrifices will please our Father.

Flesh

Romans 12:1 AMP - Therefore I urge you, brothers and sisters, by the mercies of God, to present your bodies [dedicating all of yourselves, set apart] as a living sacrifice, holy and well-pleasing to God, which is your rational (logical, intelligent) act of worship.

The first sacrifice is our flesh.

◊ **We are to become living sacrifices.** ◊

That means that although we are alive, we are dead to our own way of doing things. We are also dead to sin and its pitfalls. We choose to be guided by God's Spirit. This is a daily process. Just like the sacrifices of the Old Testament were continual, to keep the altar's fire burning, so shall we have to continually choose to live out of the Spirit and not of the flesh. Jesus Himself dealt with this same thing. He had to choose to sacrifice the human will for God's will. Since Jesus had to choose to sacrifice His flesh (in more ways than one), then we must know that we will have to choose in like manner.

SPREAD YOUR WINGS AND SOAR

> *Hebrews 7:27 CEV - and He is better than any other high priest. Jesus doesn't need to offer sacrifices each day for His own sins and then for the sins of the people. He offered a sacrifice once for all, when He gave himself.*

Every year on Yom Kippur, the Day of Atonement, the High Priest would offer a sin sacrifice for the totality of all the sins of Israel and himself. He would enter into the Holy of Holies just this one time. It was so dangerous they would tie a rope around the High Priest to pull them out if they stopped hearing their bells ring. If they made one mistake - they would die immediately because our God cannot touch anything unholy. However, much unlike the Old Testament, Jesus was able to be the sin sacrifice by offering Himself one time.

> *Hebrews 9:26 AMP - Otherwise, He would have needed to suffer over and over since the foundation of the world; but now once for all at the consummation of the ages He has appeared and been publicly manifested to put away sin by the sacrifice of Himself.*
>
> *Hebrews 10:12 CEV - But Christ offered Himself as a sacrifice that is good forever. Now He is sitting at God's right side,*

There is no need anymore for the blood of bulls, lambs, birds, and goats! Thank God, that Jesus' blood was more than enough to wash away the power, punishment, and pollution of sin once and for all! He operated as High Priest in our stead. We could never have done it. Only Jesus was able to due to His Divine nature. He has forever torn apart the veil that separated us from the mercy seat of our Father God.

Mark 15:37-38 NKJV - 37 And Jesus cried out with a loud voice, and breathed His last. 38 Then the veil of the temple was torn in two from top to bottom.

Jesus conquered sin for us. Now, through our faith in Him, we are able to conquer sin in our lives as well. In fact, we are able to rule over the flesh's wants and desires.

We have the power to choose to follow God.

What an awesome gift from God! When we come to the end of ourselves, which means that we are done trying to live life our own way, we are able to sacrifice ourselves to Him as a sweet smelling aroma to God the Father. We no longer live, but it is Christ in us. He lives our life far better than we could!

> *Galatians 2:20 ESV - I have been crucified with Christ. It is no longer I who live, but Christ Who lives in me. And the life I now live in the flesh I live by faith in the Son of God, who loved me and gave Himself for me.*

I know this sounds ridiculous to the human mind, but it makes perfect sense in the spirit. You die to self, which means you do not allow your unrenewed sinful tendencies to rule your life's decisions. Instead, you lean on, trust in, and believe in Jesus Christ and the power of the Holy Spirit to lead you in wisdom, righteousness, and love. I cannot tell you how important of a decision this is for your life! It will be one of the best decisions of your life if you truly mean it and follow through on it. For us, it is not a one-time sacrifice. We are not perfect like Jesus, but we are on our way to perfection! We choose to follow Him everyday as His anointed and set apart priests.

Emotions

The second sacrifice that is acceptable to God is your emotions. In Native American culture, the eagle was a sign of peace, and why would it not be? Eagles seem to have it all together. You do not see them flying off the handle for any little thing. They are reserved and calculated. When something happens that they do not like, they fly elsewhere. The only time they get an attitude is if you attack their nest! Like the eagle, you must sacrifice those emotions that get riled up at times. Choose to walk in love. Choose not to get offended. Choose to forgive and forget. Choose to remain calm and at peace. Be like the eagle and go away if need be. I am trying to save you from trouble.

> **Emotions are meant to enhance your life but not to lead you.**

Do not let emotions run (ruin) your life!

> *Ephesians 5:2 NKJV - And walk in love, as Christ also has loved us and given Himself for us, an offering and a sacrifice to God for a sweet-smelling aroma.*
>
> *Proverbs 15:18 MSG - Hot tempers start fights; a calm, cool spirit keeps the peace.*

You have the fruit of self-control available to you. This means that you are able to tell yourself no. You are capable of controlling your impulses.

> *Galatians 5:22-23 AMP - 22 But the fruit of the Spirit [the result of His presence within us] is love [unselfish concern for others], joy, [inner] peace, patience [not the ability to wait, but how we act while waiting], kindness, goodness, faithfulness,*

23 gentleness, self-control. Against such things there is no law.

Jesus told us to forgive those who hurt us. Even if they did it on purpose, even if they stole from you, even if they abused you, even if they hurt your loved one, even if they lied about you, and even if they betrayed your trust… forgive them!

There is no reason we cannot forgive when we compare how much we have been forgiven.

Matthew 5:43-46 CEV - 43 You have heard people say, "Love your neighbors and hate your enemies." 44 But I tell you to love your enemies and pray for anyone who mistreats you. 45 Then you will be acting like your Father in heaven. He makes the sun rise on both good and bad people. And He sends rain for the ones who do right and for the ones who do wrong. 46 If you love only those people who love you, will God reward you for this? Even tax collectors love their friends.

Look how Jesus practices what He preaches! He had every reason to be offended, but He chose to not let His emotions get the better of Him. He interceded on their behalf.

Luke 23:34-35 MSG - Jesus prayed, "Father,

> *forgive them; they don't know what they're doing." Dividing up his clothes, they threw dice for them. The people stood there staring at Jesus, and the ringleaders made faces, taunting, "He saved others. Let's see Him save himself! The Messiah of God—ha! The Chosen—ha!"*

Since Jesus was able to forgive while they crucified Him, we have no excuses. True forgiveness only comes through God. Once you know how much you have been forgiven, then you can forgive others.

> *Luke 7:47 KJV - Wherefore I say unto thee, Her sins, which are many, are forgiven; for she loved much: but to whom little is forgiven, the same loveth little.*

Praise & Thanksgiving

The third sacrifice acceptable to God is your praise and thanksgiving. Even when you do not feel like it. Even when the world is against you. Even when everyone has turned on you.

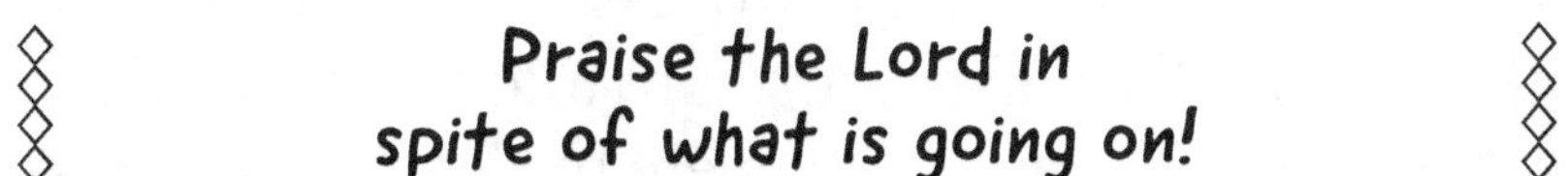

Thank Him for His goodness and kindness toward you!

SPREAD YOUR WINGS AND SOAR

> *Hebrews 13:15 AMP - Through Him, therefore, let us at all times offer up to God a sacrifice of praise, which is the fruit of lips that thankfully acknowledge and confess and glorify His name.*

It can be a challenge at times. I have had my fair share of difficult things that required me to stir up my praise. My greatest trial was losing my 20-year old son George III. Oh, what a terrible time that was for my family and me! That kind of difficulty requires you to have a knowledge of your God beforehand.

One must remember that with God there are no mistakes.

That our Creator is sovereign in all that He does. There is never a time when He slumbers or sleeps. There is never a time when things get out of His control. As I came to grips with the fact that God had allowed my son to depart this life, I then had to learn how to praise God in a hard place.

It was not an easy process, except for the fact that a loving God had chosen to allow George III. to go home at that age. There were many nights of tears and sorrow. It was hard on all of our family because he was truly dear to us. George III. had just left the house with his uncle. He was traveling to the eastside of Indianapolis, when he was shot in the head by a drive-by shooter. Within minutes he was dead. No warning or notices given. I can remember very clearly while standing in Wishard hospital and seeing my son on the Gurney. I asked God a question: "What do you want me to do?" Did He want me to believe that He would raise him up, or was this situation between him and his God. I heard God say, "It is between George III. and Me." It was at that point, I knew that I was going to have to face the realization that my son would not be with us any longer. I would have to learn what David said in Psalms 34:1.

> *Psalms 34:1 KJV - A Psalm of David, I will bless the LORD at all times: His praise shall continually be in my mouth.*

I made a decision that because of this terrible event, I was going to turn up my praise and worship to a God that had loaned my son to me for 20 years.

I have learned that no one's children are their property.

They all belong to God, and we do not know the time and the moment that they will return to Him.

We can let situations weigh us down if we let them.

◊ *We have to tell our heart how to feel.* ◊

We have to choose to focus with eyes of faith, and not remain influenced by our senses. David knew this very well.

> *Psalm 42:11 NKJV - Why are you cast down, O my soul? And why are you disquieted within me? Hope in God; For I shall yet praise Him, The help of my countenance and my God.*

He spoke to his heart to affect how he was feeling. He chose to praise God in every situation. We are to do the same.

*Give God the sacrifice of praise,
and watch Him use it for His glory!*

God is able to do amazing things when we praise Him!

3: DRESS / CONDUCT

The third duty of the priest is to dress the part. One of the definitions of majestic is, "having or showing impressive beauty or dignity." An eagle certainly fulfills this criteria. In Native American culture, eagle feathers are highly regarded and respected. To be given an eagle feather is to receive protection or great honor: like when they graduated college or are going on a long journey to a faraway country. The eagle feather will remind them that they are being watched over by their gods. In like manner, our priestly garb is highly regarded by God and demonstrates His glory. They are a sign that we belong to God Almighty and that He is watching over us. We can see that the first thing God did for Adam and Eve after they fell was to give them proper covering.

> *Genesis 3:21 KJV - Unto Adam also and to his wife did the LORD God make coats of skins, and clothed them.*

God is telling us that we must also clothe ourselves with the correct garb. For a New Testament believer, this is the character of Christ.

We wear Christ as our robe of righteousness.

We wear His blood and bear His name. We are bound together by His love. Read what Paul says about this.

> *Colossians 3:12-17 MSG - 12-14 So, chosen by God for this new life of love, dress in the*

> wardrobe God picked out for you: compassion, kindness, humility, quiet strength, discipline. Be even-tempered, content with second place, quick to forgive an offense. Forgive as quickly and completely as the Master forgave you. And regardless of what else you put on, wear love. It's your basic, all-purpose garment. Never be without it. 15-17 Let the peace of Christ keep you in tune with each other, in step with each other. None of this going off and doing your own thing. And cultivate thankfulness. Let the Word of Christ—the Message—have the run of the house. Give it plenty of room in your lives. Instruct and direct one another using good common sense. And sing, sing your hearts out to God! Let every detail in your lives—words, actions, whatever—be done in the name of the Master, Jesus, thanking God the Father every step of the way.

We dress in compassion, kindness, humility, quiet strength, and discipline. These attributes closely resemble the fruit of the Spirit from Galatians 5:22-23.

We are enveloped so much by Christ that our identity becomes inseparable from His.

> Galatians 5:22-23 KJV - 22 But the fruit of the Spirit is love, joy, peace, longsuffering, gentleness, goodness, faith, 23 Meekness, temperance: against such there is no law.

SPREAD YOUR WINGS AND SOAR

As we choose to follow Jesus, we must look and act the part as His beloved priests.

> **We want people to see Christ in us and all over us when they watch our lives.**

We are to provoke even the Jewish nation to jealousy! Jesus said that the world would recognize Him by the love that is shown between His followers.

> *John 13:35 CEV - If you love each other, everyone will know that you are My disciples.*

We also have the garments of praise in our wardrobe. Wear your garment of praise. Showcase your love for the Lord by praising and thanking Him wherever you are. He is worthy of praise!

> *Isaiah 61:3 NKJV - To console those who mourn in Zion, To give them beauty for ashes, The oil of joy for mourning, The garment of praise for the spirit of heaviness; That they may be called trees of righteousness, The planting of the LORD, that He may be glorified."*

We have the garments of salvation and the robe of righteousness. Put them on for all to see Christ in you. You have been redeemed forever by the blood of the Lamb.

> *Isaiah 61:10 NKJV - I will greatly rejoice in the LORD, My soul shall be joyful in my God; For He has clothed me with the garments of salvation, He has covered me with the robe of righteousness, As a bridegroom decks [himself] with ornaments, And as a bride adorns [herself] with her jewels.*

Who can forget that we have the Armor of God to help us stand firm in the faith.

Wear your armor. Be battle-ready at all times.

Be prepared to be deployed. God has a need for you, mighty soldier!

> *Ephesians 6:13-18 NKJV - 13 Therefore take up the whole armor of God, that you may be able to withstand in the evil day, and having done all, to stand. 14 Stand therefore, having girded your waist with truth, having put on the breastplate of righteousness, 15 and having shod your feet with the preparation of the gospel of peace; 16 above all, taking the shield of faith with which you will be able to quench all the fiery darts of the wicked one. 17 And take the helmet of salvation, and the sword of the Spirit, which is the word*

of God; 18 praying always with all prayer and supplication in the Spirit, being watchful to this end with all perseverance and supplication for all the saints--

Christ Himself has raised us from the dead; He saved us from what was our old sinful selves. We clothe ourselves in Him. We are His army. He has prepared and equipped us to be His royal priests. We are able to fulfill His commandments because of the power of the Holy Ghost that compels us to victory!

Revelation 1:5-6 AMP - 5 and from Jesus Christ, the faithful and trustworthy Witness, the Firstborn of the dead, and the Ruler of the kings of the earth. To Him who [always] loves us and who [has once for all] freed us [or washed us] from our sins by His own blood (His sacrificial death)— 6 and formed us into a kingdom [as His subjects], priests to His God and Father—to Him be the glory and the power and the majesty and the dominion forever and ever. Amen.

4: BLESS

The fourth duty of the priest is to bless the people. Encourage, exhort, build up, prophesy, and speak the Word of God to your brethren. We are in this life together to help each other. People need to hear what you have to say!

SPREAD YOUR WINGS AND SOAR

> *Numbers 6:23-27 NKJV - 23 "Speak to Aaron and his sons, saying, Thus you shall bless the people of Israel: you shall say to them, 24 The Lord bless you and keep you; 25 the Lord make his face to shine upon you and be gracious to you; 26 the Lord lift up his countenance upon you and give you peace. 27 "So shall they put my name upon the people of Israel, and I will bless them."*

We are gifts to one another. The gifts that we have are to be used for others' well-being. We should help a brother or sister out when we see a need. We are not islands.

We are precious brothers and sisters in Christ.

Human beings are innately social. We rely on communication with others around us. God knew this! He created us like this! We must treasure one another as the gifts we are from God to each other.

> *Romans 12:6-9 AMP - 6 Since we have gifts that differ according to the grace given to us, each of us is to use them accordingly: if [someone has the gift of] prophecy, [let him speak a new message from God to His people] in proportion to the faith possessed; 7 if service, in the act of serving; or he who teaches, in the act of teaching; 8 or he*

> *who encourages, in the act of encouragement; he who gives, with generosity; he who leads, [a] with diligence; he who shows mercy [in caring for others], with cheerfulness. 9 Love is to be sincere and active [the real thing—without guile and hypocrisy]. Hate what is evil [detest all ungodliness, do not tolerate wickedness]; hold on tightly to what is good.*

You are blessed therefore you are a blessing. Let us serve each other with joy: esteeming one another above ourselves. Bless your friends, bless your families, and bless your enemies; speak forth God's Word, and be amazed at the transformations that will occur in their lives. Thank God, we have been given this wonderful privilege to bless others!

> *1 Peter 4:11 CEV - If you have the gift of speaking, preach God's message. If you have the gift of helping others, do it with the strength that God supplies. Everything should be done in a way that will bring honor to God because of Jesus Christ, who is glorious and powerful forever. Amen.*

TABERNACLE IN THE WILDERNESS

A priest has a jurisdiction where their responsibilities are carried out. The majority of eagles have a specific area where they live. They choose to stay in their local environment because it satisfies all of their needs. They know the area well and are comfortable. For the Old Testament priests, they could only minister in and around the Tabernacle and then later in Solomon's Temple. These are the places where they carried out their duties. Let us compare the similarities of the Tabernacle to our relationship with God from the New Covenant perspective.

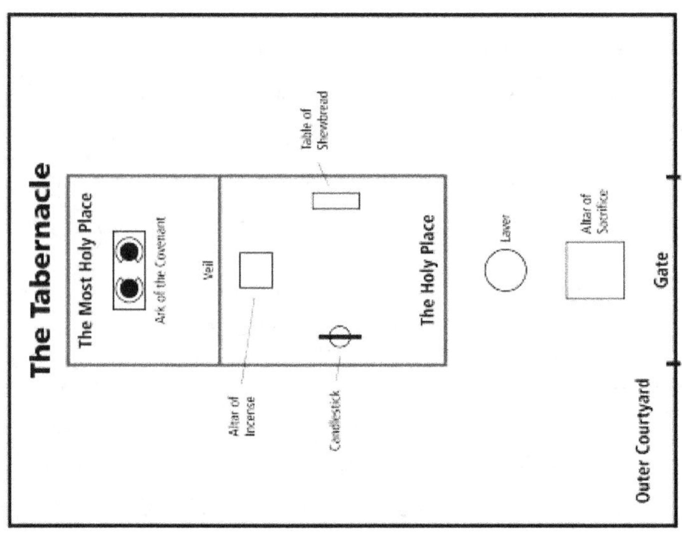

EAST AND WEST

Starting out, the progression toward the Tabernacle is from East to West. This is indicative of the distance between the holy and the unholy. David had a poetic way of describing this.

> *Psalms 103:12 KJV - As far as the east is from the west, so far hath He removed our transgressions from us.*

Another meaning we can derive from this is that the Sun rises in the East and sets in the West.

Jesus is our Righteous Star that points us toward God and leads us further from sin.

We know this because Jesus is called the Bright and Morning Star in Revelation.

> *Revelation 22:16 KJV - I Jesus have sent mine angel to testify unto you these things in the churches. I am the root and the offspring of David, and the bright and morning star.*

Stars are not typically seen in the morning (besides the Sun). They are not visible due to being outshined by the Sun. When the Sun goes down, then the stars have a chance to be seen. Jesus is such a Bright Star that the rest of the stars pale in comparison to His glory. He outshines them all. He can be seen no matter what the time or season dictates. He so outshines sin that it is no longer in the picture.

SPREAD YOUR WINGS AND SOAR

> *Colossians 1:14 AMP - in whom we have redemption [because of His sacrifice, resulting in] the forgiveness of our sins [and the cancellation of sins' penalty].*

ENTER HIS GATES WITH THANKSGIVING

Next, we come to the gates. The gates represent the entrance into God's presence. The way to open the gates is with thanksgiving. The way we enter into God's manifest presence starts with thanksgiving.

Thank God for all the wonderful things He has done for you.

If you cannot think of a single thing, then thank God for sending Jesus to save you! That should be more than enough to stir up your praise.

> *Psalms 100:4a KJV - Enter into His gates with thanksgiving*

Another way we can look at this is that Jesus said that He is the Gate.

> *John 10:9 CEV - I am the Gate. All who come in through Me will be saved. Through Me they will come and go and find pasture.*

We come to Jesus with thanksgiving for all that He has done for us. We enter into His presence. We find our rest and peace in Him. It all starts with thanksgiving.

COME INTO THE COURTS WITH PRAISE

Next up, we come to the courts. The courts are a deeper relationship with God. Your thanksgiving brings you to a place of praise. You are coming closer to His throne room. The courts are where the duties are carried out. Your reasonable service should always be done with thanksgiving that leads to praise.

> *Psalms 100:4b KJV - and into His courts with praise: be thankful unto Him, and bless His name.*

Look at how in the Psalms they longed to be close to God. The courts were the closest proximity some people could ever get to the Lord, and yet they desired to know Him. The praises of God could be heard in His courts.

> *Psalms 84:1-12 ESV - 1 How lovely is Your dwelling place, O Lord of Hosts! 2 My soul longs, yes, faints for the courts of the Lord; my heart and flesh sing for joy to the living God. 3 Even the sparrow finds a home, and the swallow a nest*

for herself, where she may lay her young, at your altars, O Lord of Hosts, my King and my God. 4 Blessed are those who dwell in Your house, ever singing Your praise! Selah 5 Blessed are those whose strength is in You, in whose heart are the highways to Zion. 6 As they go through the Valley of Baca they make it a place of springs; the early rain also covers it with pools.7 They go from strength to strength; each one appears before God in Zion. 8 O Lord God of Hosts, hear my prayer; give ear, O God of Jacob! Selah 9 Behold our shield, O God; look on the face of Your anointed! 10 For a day in Your courts is better than a thousand elsewhere. I would rather be a doorkeeper in the house of my God than dwell in the tents of wickedness. 11 For the Lord God is a Sun and Shield; the Lord bestows favor and honor. No good thing does He withhold from those who walk uprightly. 12 O Lord of Hosts, blessed is the one who trusts in You!

BE WASHED BY THE WORD

Next, before a priest could handle any sacrifices or even go into the tabernacle, they had to wash in the basin. This signifies that we are cleansed of unrighteousness by the blood of Jesus. We choose to wash ourselves by the renewing of His Word that leads us to repentance. We repent (change our mind) and confess our shortcomings to the Lord and receive refreshment in His presence.

SPREAD YOUR WINGS AND SOAR

> *Ephesians 5:26 KJV - That He might sanctify and cleanse it with the washing of water by the Word,*

As we come before Him with our hearts washed of all iniquity, we are able to proceed boldly and commit ourselves to doing the work that He has called us to do.

> *1 Corinthians 6:9-11 CEV - 9 Don't you know that evil people won't have a share in the blessings of God's kingdom? Don't fool yourselves! No one who is immoral or worships idols or is unfaithful in marriage or is a pervert or behaves like a homosexual 10 will share in God's kingdom. Neither will any thief or greedy person or drunkard or anyone who curses and cheats others. 11 Some of you used to be like that. But now the name of our Lord Jesus Christ and the power of God's Spirit have washed you and made you holy and acceptable to God.*

BRING YOUR SACRIFICE TO THE ALTAR

Next, we take our sacrifice, offering, gift, oblation, or what have you to the door of the tabernacle next to the bronze altar. Bronze represents judgment. Every sacrifice we bring is judged by God.

God cannot accept an unholy or imperfect offering.

He is looking for a pure heart that is devoted to Him. The sacrifice must be inspected and approved by a priest. Once the sacrifice is approved, the priest prepares our sacrifice, and offers it on the altar to be burned up as a sweet-smelling aroma to God.

> *Hebrews 4:12-13 NKJV - 12 For the Word of God [is] living and powerful, and sharper than any two-edged sword, piercing even to the division of soul and spirit, and of joints and marrow, and is a discerner of the thoughts and intents of the heart. 13 And there is no creature hidden from His sight, but all things [are] naked and open to the eyes of Him to whom we [must give] account.*

We previously mentioned that our New Testament sacrifices can be our flesh, our emotions, or our praise and thanksgiving. We are giving to the Lord out of our substance. We are giving Him our heart and allowing Him to judge us. We know that God is the one who judges the intent of the heart. We demonstrate our adoration to the Lord by offering these sacrifices which bring forth His aroma of goodness in our lives.

> *2 Corinthians 2:14-16 AMP - 14 But thanks be to God, who always leads us in triumph in Christ, and through us spreads and makes evident everywhere the sweet fragrance of the knowledge*

of Him. 15 For we are the sweet fragrance of Christ [which ascends] to God, [discernible both] among those who are being saved and among those who are perishing; 16 to the latter one an aroma from death to death [a fatal, offensive odor], but to the other an aroma from life to life [a vital fragrance, living and fresh].

HIGH PRIEST

For the High Priest, there is also much symbolism that relates to our walk with God.

Table of Showbread

Inside of the Tabernacle there is the Table of Showbread. This represents the Word of God that sustains us. This is our daily bread. Each morning new bread was made and laid out. Bread is made of grains which are carbohydrates. Carbohydrates release energy over time. We get our sustaining energy from the Word of God that we partake in each day. It is fresh everyday. This is why they had to collect manna everyday (except on the Sabbath) because God would not allow His people to live on previous stale revelations. He wants to reveal Himself in new ways every single day through His Word.

Colossians 1:15-18 CEV - 15 Christ is exactly like God, who cannot be seen. He is the first-born

Son, superior to all creation.16 Everything was created by him, everything in heaven and on earth, everything seen and unseen, including all forces and powers, and all rulers and authorities. All things were created by God's Son, and everything was made for Him.17 God's Son was before all else, and by Him everything is held together.18 He is the head of His body, which is the church. He is the very beginning, the first to be raised from death, so that He would be above all others.

Golden Candlestick Lampstand

Inside of the Tabernacle there is the Golden Candlestick Lampstand. This is the light of truth: God's justice that shines in the dark. It was the only source of light in the entire enclosure.

⬧ **We are living in the light of Christ's goodness.** ⬧

He reveals the way for us. The shadows that would deceive us are made manifest by His light.

Psalm 119:105 KJV - Thy Word is a Lamp unto my feet, and a Light unto my path.

John 3:21 CEV - But everyone who lives by the truth will come to the light, because they want others to know that God is really the One doing what they do.

The lampstand had seven almond blossom heads which represent the seven spirits of God. The almonds signify that God is watching over His Word to perform it. The reason is that the almond is one of the first trees to bloom when the season is right. In God's timing, His Word will bloom quickly!

Isaiah 11:1-2 NKJV - 1 There shall come forth a Rod from the stem of Jesse, And a Branch shall grow out of his roots. 2 The Spirit of the LORD shall rest upon Him, The Spirit of wisdom and understanding, The Spirit of counsel and might, The Spirit of knowledge and of the fear of the LORD.

Jeremiah 1:11-12 NKJV - 11 Moreover the word of the LORD came to me, saying, "Jeremiah, what do you see?" And I said, "I see a branch of an almond tree." 12 Then the LORD said to me, "You have seen well, for I AM ready to perform My Word."

Gold represents value.

We must value the truth of God's Word in our lives!

The Spirit of Truth, the Holy Spirit, will teach and instruct us as we value Him. Value His wisdom above all else!

John 16:13 AMP - But when He, the Spirit of Truth, comes, He will guide you into all the truth [full and complete truth]. For He will not speak on His own initiative, but He will speak whatever He hears [from the Father—the message regarding the Son], and He will disclose to you what is to come [in the future].

Proverbs 4:7 KJV - Wisdom [is] the principal thing; [therefore] get wisdom: and with all thy getting get understanding.

Altar of Incense

The Altar of Incense represents our prayer life. Our prayers to God and our communication with Him, fills up the incense and becomes a sweet aromatic offering. Every morning, new incense was put out for God. In the same way, we are to have a consistent prayer life that begins in the morning. As long you are awake then your prayer life should be active!

Exodus 30:7-8 AMP - 7 Aaron shall burn sweet and fragrant incense on it; he shall burn it every morning when he trims and tends the lamps. 8 When Aaron sets up the lamps at twilight, he shall burn incense, a perpetual incense before the Lord throughout your generations.

1 Chronicles 23:30 CEV - Every morning and evening, the Levites are to give thanks to the Lord and sing praises to Him.

Veil

There was a curtain (veil) that would separate the Holiest of Holies from the rest of the Tabernacle. It was sewn out of the finest linens of blue, purple, and red wool then embroidered with cherubim (winged-angelic creatures). This curtain could only be entered into once a year on the day of atonement by the High Priest. It represents the sinful nature of man that could not approach a holy God. We would still be stuck in sin had it not been for Jesus! Only through Jesus, who tore the veil from top to bottom, could enter in and make us holy by His blood.

Matthew 27:51 KJV - And, behold, the veil of the temple was rent in twain from the top to the bottom; and the earth did quake, and the rocks rent;

Holy of Holies

The Holy of Holies was the chamber that contained the Ark of the Covenant (chest), the mercy seat resting on top of the chest, and two cherubim that covered the mercy seat with their wings. Inside of the Ark of the Covenant were three things: the tablets of testimony, the bloomed rod (almond blossom) of Aaron, and a vessel of manna. These represent the written Law of God, the authority of God's Word, and the provision of God's Word. As I have mentioned several times, only on the Day of Atonement could the High Priest enter into the Holy of Holies. Jesus Christ, our Savior, chose to be our High Priest.

He offered Himself once and for all to cover for our sin nature and to blot out our sins.

Hebrews 7:23-28 MSG - 23-25 Earlier there were a lot of priests, for they died and had to be replaced. But Jesus' priesthood is permanent. He's there from now to eternity to save everyone who comes to God through Him, always on the job to speak up for them. 26-28 So now we have a high priest who perfectly fits our needs: completely holy, uncompromised by sin, with authority extending as high as God's presence in heaven itself. Unlike the other high priests, He

> *doesn't have to offer sacrifices for his own sins every day before He can get around to us and our sins. He's done it, once and for all: offered up Himself as the sacrifice. The law appoints as high priests men who are never able to get the job done right. But this intervening command of God, which came later, appoints the Son, who is absolutely, eternally perfect.*

Jesus has given us access to the throne room of God. We are now, new creations completely set apart and holy unto God. He traded His righteousness for our sinful nature: the great exchange! We are now able to know God personally and intimately. We can know Him as our Father. We are able to receive the blessings of God because we are in His family, and God treats His family very well!

> *2 Corinthians 5:21 AMP - He made Christ who knew no sin to [judicially] be sin on our behalf, so that in Him we would become the righteousness of God [that is, we would be made acceptable to Him and placed in a right relationship with Him by His gracious lovingkindness].*

> *Romans 8:15-17 MSG - This resurrection life you received from God is not a timid, grave-tending life. It's adventurously expectant, greeting God with a childlike "What's next, Papa?" God's Spirit touches our spirits and confirms who we*

> *really are. We know who He is, and we know who we are: Father and children. And we know we are going to get what's coming to us—an unbelievable inheritance! We go through exactly what Christ goes through. If we go through the hard times with Him, then we're certainly going to go through the good times with Him!*

TABERNACLE SUMMARY

The Tabernacle is a perfect representation of our life in God today. His Word is our bread. His truth is our light.

Our prayers are a sweet-smelling aroma unto Him.

We can enter boldly and entreat the mercy seat of God whenever we desire; for the veil has been removed by the blood of Jesus Christ.

> *Hebrews 4:16 CEV - So whenever we are in need, we should come bravely before the throne of our merciful God. There we will be treated with undeserved grace, and we will find help.*

WE ARE LIVING TEMPLES

Today, as God's priests, we can see that there are places we are called to minister. This could be in our families, at work, at school, at church, or anywhere the Lord leads. We are the temples of His Holy Spirit.

1 Corinthians 3:16 KJV - Know ye not that ye are the temple of God, and that the Spirit of God dwelleth in you?

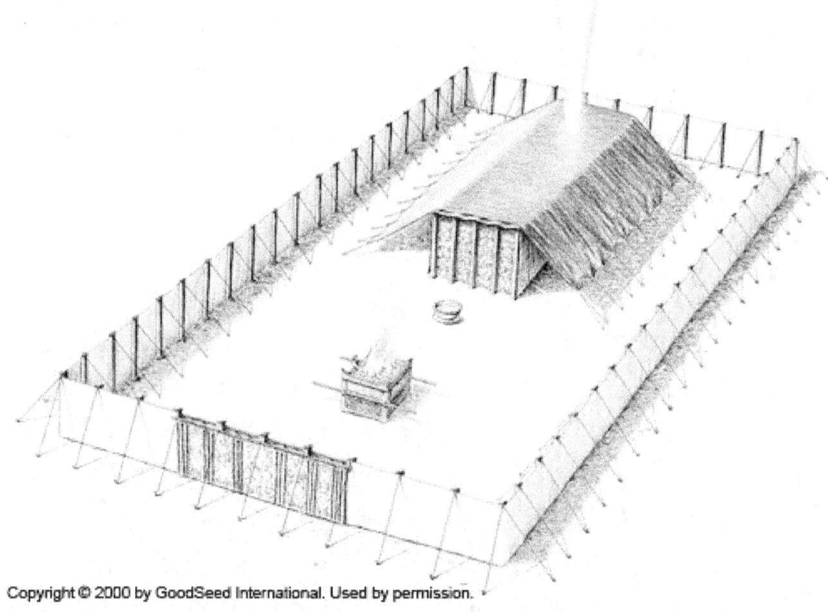

We are able to minister anywhere we go; for the presence of God is always with us. We choose to heed His voice and share His love with all those around us.

> **We are equipped and called
> to make disciples of Jesus.**

Let us go forth and do as Jesus asked of us. We are equipped to do it!

> *Matthew 28:18-20 CEV - 18 Jesus came to them and said: I have been given all authority in heaven and on earth! 19 Go to the people of all nations and make them My disciples. Baptize them in the name of the Father, the Son, and the Holy Spirit, 20 and teach them to do everything I have told you. I will be with you always, even until the end of the world.*

SUMMARY

In summary, you are a holy and royal priest unto God. You are called to pray, make sacrifices, bless others, and wear Christ. You are able to come close to God for fellowship, and to minister unto Him. God Himself has qualified you with the blood of His Son! You are holy because God has said you are holy. His Word is your daily food. You are equipped because you have the Holy Spirit to guide you in truth. Your prayer life is your incense before the Lord. You are able to boldly come to the mercy seat and ask for grace as much and as often as you would like. You are able to minister to God wherever you are. Rule over your territory - you majestic eagle.

PRAYER

Father God, in the precious name of Jesus, we come to You. Help us to see that we are Your priests. Help us to know that we are Your royal priesthood set apart from the foundations of the Earth, to give You glory and praise, and to serve You with a humble heart. We choose this day to take on our responsibilities as priests. We shall offer the sacrifice of our flesh, emotions, prayer and thanksgiving as sweet-smelling perfume to You.

Help us to remain in the proper mindset. We shall wear our priestly garments, boldly, being ever ready to receive orders from You. We ask You to show us where we need to use our giftings. We give You praise for doing it. In Jesus' awesome name we pray. Amen.

CHAPTER 5

TWO SETS OF VISION

EAGLES SEE THE BEST

The Aboriginal people have what is called, "super vision." They can see four-times greater than the average human. Scientists could not see the star formations that were written about until telescopes were used. Then, they could understand what the Aborigines were talking about. For them, they need superior vision to hunt in the wild. With their excellent eyes, they are able to aim further with their hunting weapons ensuring they will have food for the day. Much like the eagle, having superior vision helps them survive.

I am sure you have heard of the term, "eagle eyes," or, "eagle vision." The eyes of the eagle are no joke. They are some of the strongest in the animal kingdom. What most people do not know is that they have two sets of vision. They can see forward and sideways at the same time with a field-of-vision that spreads 340 degrees. They have 20/5 vision, which means that what looks sharp and clear to us at five-feet is just as clear to an eagle from 20 feet away. They can survey an area of three square miles flying at an altitude of about 1,000 feet. That is some serious range!

AN EAGLE COULD SEE:

- A 2-millimeter insect from 60 feet away
- A mouse from 446 feet away
- An ant from the top of a ten-story building
- The faces of basketball players from the back of a large arena
- A rabbit from over three miles away

YOU HAVE TWO SETS OF VISION

Compared to eagles, we also have two sets of vision: the natural and the spiritual. We should be desiring to see more with our spiritual vision than our physical vision. Let us look at this example from scripture.

> *2 Kings 6:15-17 ESV - 15 When the servant of the man of God rose early in the morning and went out, behold, an army with horses and chariots was all around the city. And the servant said, "Alas, my master! What shall we do?" 16 He said, "Do not be afraid, for those who are with us are more than those who are with them." 17 Then Elisha prayed and said, "O Lord, please open his eyes that he may see." So the Lord opened the eyes of the young man, and he saw, and behold, the mountain was full of horses and chariots of fire all around Elisha.*

The servant was only able to see the physical circumstance: not the spiritual answer. We would have a much more drama-free life if we had 20/20 spiritual vision. Our soul must be trained to observe both the spiritual and the physical.

Emotionally-controlled people have not developed their spiritual vision.

There is no such thing as an emotional person per se. God has given us all emotions, but He wants us in control of them, not them controlling us. Emotions give us our personalities and make us unique, but they are meant to enhance, not control. We can respond to situations with emotion, but we should never respond out of emotion.

PERSPECTIVE

With proper vision, you must also have a proper perspective. Perspective could be defined as, "the faculty of seeing all the relevant data in a meaningful relationship."

> Just as we must develop our spiritual eyesight, our perspective must be from the right vantage point.

It would do the eagle no good to have such amazing eyesight and never leave the ground. What good is it to have the ability to see a rabbit three miles away if it cannot see out of the forest it is sitting in? When the eagle flies, it can find what it needs more easily. For our vision to see the answer, we have to get to a place where we can get God's perspective. Our eyes will never see the answer if we are looking up at our problem rather than looking down on our problem from our position of righteousness.

Ephesians 2:4-6 ESV - 4 But God, being rich in mercy, because of the great love with which He loved us, 5 even when we were dead in our trespasses, made us alive together with Christ— by grace you have been saved— 6 and raised us up with Him and seated us with Him in the heavenly places in Christ Jesus.

Make sure to look at the big picture. You have the victory in Jesus. To demonstrate this, read this letter that a young woman from college sent to her parents.

Dear Mom and Dad,
Just thought I'd drop you a note to clue you in on my plans. I've fallen in love with a guy named Jim. He quit high school after grade eleven to get married. About a year ago he got a divorce. We've been going steady for two months and plan to get married in the fall. Until then, I've decided to move into his apartment (I think I might be pregnant). At any rate, I dropped out of school last week, although I'd like to finish college sometime in the future.

On the next page she continued:

Mom and Dad, I just want you to know that everything I've written so far in this letter is false. NONE of it is true. But Mom and Dad, it IS true that I got a C in French and flunked Math. It IS also true that I'm going to need some more money for my tuition payments.

As this letter points out, it could always be

worse, and our perspective on things plays a big part in how boldly we approach our circumstances. When we get God's view, from the right hand of authority on high, we will see that our answer is much closer than we thought.

> The solution will be plainly seen with our spiritual vision when we have the correct vantage point.

DISCERNMENT

Eagles must be able to discern the things they see. They can with their 1,000,000 cones in their retinas that allow them to see brighter colors and even the ultraviolet spectrum. They also have an oil that is in their cone receptor cells that filters out harmful light and enhances color. They can detect color shades much better than we can. They must… for their survival depends on how well they hunt. Discernment could be defined as, "acuteness of judgment and understanding, insight." When we get our vision developed and the proper perspective, we will learn that we will have to discern between several, "answers," that may come into view.

> Romans 12:2 ESV - Do not be conformed to this world, but be transformed by the renewal of your

> *mind, that by testing you may discern what is the will of God, what is good and acceptable and perfect.*

As an eagle flies and hunts, it may see several food options, but certain things will be better for the nest like fish, rabbits, snakes and dead things. All could be considered a food source, but not all are as beneficial as some others. In fact, some are actually harmful. The first, "answer," you see, may not be the right or best answer.

⚜   **Good things are not always God things.**   ⚜

There are different levels of God's will: good, acceptable, and perfect. Any of these are viable options, but there are greater benefits with perfect than with good or acceptable. C's are acceptable, but A's are perfect and come with more benefits and opportunities. Aspirin is good, but healing is perfect. If we want to soar, then we must learn to see things from a heavenly perspective. We will never become who we are ultimately called to be by walking around in a low place not seeing the big picture of what He has for us.

WHAT DOES THE BIBLE SAY ABOUT OUR EYES?

The Bible has much to say about our spiritual eyes. Let us hear what the Spirit is telling us. Read below for examples.

WALK IN THE SPIRIT

Ecclesiastes 1:8 CEV - All of life is far more boring than words could ever say. Our eyes and our ears are never satisfied with what we see and hear.

I am telling you from experience that our physical senses will wear us out. They will mislead us. They will get us all confused and they will always want more. They do not understand the whole picture. We must understand that there are more important matters than what our senses tell us.

We need to be walking in the spirit to see what is truly happening.

We should choose to see with God's eyes more than our own.

DO NOT BE LIKE EVE

Genesis 3:4-7 MSG - 4-5 The serpent told the Woman, "You won't die. God knows that the moment you eat from that tree, you'll see what's really going on. You'll be just like God, knowing everything, ranging all the way from good to evil." 6 When the Woman saw that the tree looked like good eating and realized what she would get out of it—she'd know everything!—she took and ate the fruit and then gave some to her husband, and he ate. 7 Immediately the two of them did "see what's really going on"—saw themselves naked! They sewed fig leaves together as makeshift clothes for themselves

Oh, Eve… but can we blame her? What would we have done? Can we each honestly say we would not have been tempted? In the midst of the Garden of Eden, she could see the tree from anywhere she was. How long did it take for the tree to allure her? The problem is that she was led by her eyes more than her faith. She saw the beauty of the tree. She saw that the serpent was alive. She felt like she was blinded from the truth and thought the only way to check was to eat of the tree.

> We have to be careful not to allow our senses to dictate what we believe or hold to be true.

Do not be like Eve, or you will be deceived.

DO NOT LET YOUR PHYSICAL EYES BLOCK YOUR SPIRITUAL VISION

Proverbs 29:18 MSG - If people can't see what God is doing, they stumble all over themselves; But when they attend to what He reveals, they are most blessed.

Do not let your spiritual vision be blinded by the glare of what your physical eyes see. Have you ever tried driving and the sun is right in your eyes? You cannot see well. Even with sunglasses on you will divert your gaze. Your eyes cannot handle the light of the Sun. When that light hits a reflective surface, it causes a glare that can blind you temporarily. You have to look away or change your position so that the light no longer is in your way.

There are times when we have to reposition ourselves in God. We have to choose to walk by faith. We cannot let our physical vision cast such a strong glare that our spiritual vision cannot look past it. We have got to move away from whatever is causing the glare. God is not a mystery to us. He does not want us to be ignorant of what He is doing. He has revealed His will to us through His Word.

SPREAD YOUR WINGS AND SOAR

*If we lack understanding, then
we need to ask for wisdom.*

We are His children and He is our Father. He will guide us when we walk by faith in Him. Choose to see with eyes of faith today.

LOOK UP

Genesis 22:13 MSG - Abraham looked up. He saw a ram caught by its horns in the thicket. Abraham took the ram and sacrificed it as a burnt offering instead of his son.

Abraham looked up. How important it is for us to look up at God and not down! Looking up or forward allows us to see further. Have you noticed when someone is looking down that they are worried, fearful, or burdened? It is like a heavy weight is on their shoulders. We have all been there before, but the lifter of our heads is our God! He will help our spiritual eyes see clearly as we trust Him. We look to the hills for we know where our help comes from!

FAITH HAS A LOOK

Acts 3:4 KJV - And Peter, fastening his eyes upon him with John, said, Look on us.

Your spiritual eyes see with faith. Faith has a distinct look about it. You can recognize faith. Faith is unwavering. Faith is ready to receive. Faith declares that God is faithful no matter how long it takes to manifest what you are believing for in the natural.

> **Faith sends forth praise to God, knowing that the victory is already set.**

Faith looks up to God in expectation. Look up to God and receive what you are believing!

SEE WITH FAITH

1 John 2:15-17 ESV - 15 Do not love the world or the things in the world. If anyone loves the world, the love of the Father is not in him. 16 For all that is in the world—the desires of the flesh and the desires of the eyes and pride of life—is not from the Father but is from the world. 17 And the world is passing away along with its desires, but whoever does the will of God abides forever.

The things that we see around us will pass away. They will fade into obscurity. 100's of years from now (if Jesus tarries) none of the things you see will be around. We must not let our desire for pleasure outweigh the eternal destiny God has placed inside of us. We must not get distracted away from the truth of God's Word.

Use your faith to imagine what God has said and see it come to pass in your life. How would you act if you were healed? How would you act if you were financially blessed? How would you act if the situation works out? See with eyes of faith, and you will shorten the manifestation period.

PICTURE THE PROMISE COMPLETED

Genesis 13:10,14 ESV - 10 And Lot lifted up his eyes and saw that the Jordan Valley was well watered everywhere like the garden of the Lord, like the land of Egypt, in the direction of Zoar. (This was before the Lord destroyed Sodom and Gomorrah.) ... 14 The Lord said to Abram, after Lot had separated from him, "Lift up your eyes and look from the place where you are, northward and southward and eastward and westward,

Lot, very much like Eve, was more satisfied with His physical senses than his faith in God. Did Lot do his homework? Did he check out the place he was going to? Did he jump because he liked the layout of the land as compared to the other side? We do not know, but we can see the result was not a good one for him or his family.

On the other side, Abraham was having a conversation with God. He trusted God as His source. God was trying to get Abraham to imagine what his inheritance was going to look like. God wanted him to see with eyes of faith unlike Lot. God was giving Abraham the courage to use his spiritual vision to picture the promise of God as completed. We can do the same today. We can picture the promise of God completed in our lives. How would you act if you saw it right today?

> Spiritual vision is about seeing the promises of God as if they were in front of you at this very moment.

Whatever you are believing for: be fully persuaded like Abraham, and you will see it come to pass.

BE NOT BLINDED BY UNTHANKFULNESS

> *Numbers 11:6 AMP - But now our appetite is gone; there is nothing at all [in the way of food] to be seen but this manna."*

The Israelites were blinded by their vision: having eyes but not seeing. God was providing food for them, but they grew tired of it. They stopped recognizing the blessing. Never take for granted what

God has done in your life. That is what happened here. The Israelites took God for granted. They did not recognize how awesome it was that they had a supernatural provision from God. We cannot allow our circumstances to make us forget what God has done. We must be ever thankful, ever praising Him, and ever humbled before Him. He did not have to take care of them, but He wanted to. He did not have to send Jesus, but it was His desire for us to be His family. We are forever at His mercy. It is because of Christ that we have anything to boast about. Let us continue bringing God the sacrifice of praise; for He is well able to deliver us from the hand of the enemy, and He is well able to snatch us from the jaws of defeat.

⧫ **We are victors in Him today and forevermore!** ⧫

DO NOT BE BLINDED BY SATAN

> *2 Corinthians 4:4 AMP - among them the god of this world [Satan] has blinded the minds of the unbelieving to prevent them from seeing the illuminating light of the gospel of the glory of Christ, who is the image of God.*

Satan would like nothing more than to keep us all from seeing Jesus. The world will reject us because we are not of it. We are travelers passing through until we make it to our destination. Satan will turn the entire world against you; but fear not, for Christ has the victory! Satan will prevent them from seeing the truth. Even if the truth is completely obvious, they could be blind to it. However, do not stop speaking the truth.

It is the truth that we share in Christ that will set people free.

Go set someone free with the truth of God's Word.

SEE JESUS

Isaiah 44:18 ESV - They know not, nor do they discern, for He has shut their eyes, so that they cannot see, and their hearts, so that they cannot understand.

Matthew 13:15 CEV - All of them have stubborn minds! They refuse to listen; they cover their eyes. They cannot see or hear or understand. If they could, they would turn to Me, and I would heal them."

The religious political groups of the day had their mind's eye blinded. You could say their hearts were not able to see Jesus. They were more worried about other things like prestige, money, fame, honor, and religious traditions than seeing Jesus. Sadly, there are still people and ministries that are caught up in all that. So many things in this life will distract us from Jesus. We have to have single-mindedness. We need to seek Jesus above all else.

> *Matthew 17:8 KJV - And when they had lifted up their eyes, they saw no man, save Jesus only.*

See Jesus! It is a good place to be when you can see Jesus! He will lead you. He will help you. He will show you the way. Look at Jesus and be drawn to Him. See what He is doing, and follow in like manner. See what He ignores and do the same. See how He interacts with others and mimic Him. We can learn everything we need by seeing Jesus!

JESUS CAN OPEN YOUR EYES

> *John 9:10-12 ESV - 10 So they said to him, "Then how were your eyes opened?" 11 He answered, "The man called Jesus made mud and anointed my eyes and said to me, 'Go to Siloam and wash.' So I went and washed and received my sight." 12 They said to him, "Where is He?" He said, "I do not know."*

Jesus opened his eyes. Jesus is the only One who can open our eyes. He provided the substance that this man needed. Jesus gave Him exactly what would help him. We are able to receive whatever we need from Jesus. He is the One who has opened our eyes to see His glory, His goodness, and His grace. Now that we have seen who He is, we are no longer satisfied with the natural. We want the supernatural that only He can give us! When we go to where we are sent (Siloam means, "sent."), we can get the blessing. When we follow what Jesus has asked us to do, the blessing must come. Obedience leads to blessing.

> Be obedient and do what Jesus
> has asked you to do.

He is trying to get a blessing to you!

JESUS HAS GIVEN US HIS VISION

Acts 9:18 CEV - Suddenly something like fish scales fell from Saul's eyes, and he could see. He got up and was baptized.

Ephesians 1:18 AMP - And [I pray] that the eyes of your heart [the very center and core of your being] may be enlightened [flooded with light by the Holy Spirit], so that you will know and cherish the hope [the divine guarantee, the confident expectation] to which He has called you, the riches of His glorious inheritance in the saints (God's people),

SPREAD YOUR WINGS AND SOAR

> *1 Peter 2:9 CEV - But you are God's chosen and special people. You are a group of royal priests and a holy nation. God has brought you out of darkness into His marvelous light. Now you must tell all the wonderful things He has done. The Scriptures say,*

Before Jesus, we were blind; we could not see with proper perspective. We needed an experience with Jesus to transform our vision. Paul's scales were like a set of armor over his heart. Paul was disarmed. He could no longer hold up a defense when He saw who Jesus was. When you see Jesus, your heart's walls will fall down just like Jericho's did. He will enter in and make His abode in you. He will take your heart to the kingdom of light, and then you will be able to understand. The Holy Spirit will open the eyes of your understanding to comprehend who Jesus is.

⋄ **We can see because of Jesus!** ⋄

SUMMARY 

In summary, oh that our eyes might be opened!

> *Matthew 20:29-34 ESV - 29 And as they went out of Jericho, a great crowd followed Him. 30 And behold, there were two blind men sitting*

by the roadside, and when they heard that Jesus was passing by, they cried out, "Lord, have mercy on us, Son of David!" 31 The crowd rebuked them, telling them to be silent, but they cried out all the more, "Lord, have mercy on us, Son of David!" 32 And stopping, Jesus called them and said, "What do you want Me to do for you?" 33 They said to Him, "Lord, let our eyes be opened." 34 And Jesus in pity touched their eyes, and immediately they recovered their sight and followed Him.

Do you want to see? You must have a desire to see with your spiritual eyes. Spiritual sight is necessary for you to go where God needs you. The eagle with their superior vision is able to see the currents that will take them where they want to go. They can even see beyond the surface of the water to catch what they need. Desire to see. Desire to study His Word. His currents will line up with the Bible. God wants you to see what He is doing! You will only fulfill God's plan in your life by seeing with eyes of faith. Have the vision of the eagle. See with your spiritual eyes. Look from the proper perspective and vantage point of Christ's victory. See with your spiritual eyes - you vigilant eagle.

PRAYER 

Father God, we humbly come before You. We want to see You! Jesus, open our eyes! We do not want to be swayed by our physical senses. We want to be fully convinced of the hope of our calling. We want to know You more Jesus! Help us to use our spiritual eyes to see with Your vision. We want to see from Your perspective and from Your vantage point. We thank You for transferring us from darkness to light. We choose to walk by faith, and to walk in the light of Your love that leads us safely through. We give You praise that we can see clearly with our spiritual eyes. In the name of Jesus we pray. Amen.

CHAPTER 6

VERY PATIENT

PATIENT PREDATORS

Eagles are known to be patient birds. They wait for their prey. They also wait for the perfect moment to ride storm currents. They have no trouble waiting around, but while they are waiting, they are not doing nothing; they are vigilant, ever watching, and looking at their surroundings. We should be like the eagle and have patience.

Why is patience so important to the Christian believer? Let us take a look at patience as defined in the dictionary. The meaning found was, "The ability to accept or tolerate delays, problems, or sufferings without becoming anxious." How often do you find yourself anxious? If we are always anxious, that means we are not being patient. The enemy wants us to look into ourselves and think, "Oh, I got this!" He wants to deceive you into thinking that you can solve every problem that comes your way without God. We need God! We will quickly find ourselves saying, "I really do not have this!" We need to be totally dependent upon God.

In scripture, patience is described as endurance. One of the first things that comes to mind when hearing the word, "endurance," is someone running a race. Some may view life as a race. I understand that, but you should only see life as a race if you see God standing at the finish line waiting for you with arms wide open as you enter Heaven! Otherwise, I personally do not think we should view life as a race, because we will miss all of the wonderful things God has in store for us here on Earth. God has created some beautiful things here on the Earth for us to see and enjoy!

> *James 1:2-3 NKJV - 2 My brethren, count it all joy when you fall into various trials, 3 knowing that the testing of your faith produces patience.*

We have to press through some things in order for patience to be complete in us. We have to learn to trust God in a variety of trials so we can be all that He needs us to be. He is forming and shaping us into what He wants us to be!

> *Isaiah 64:8 ESV - But now, O Lord, you are our Father; we are the clay, and You are our potter; we are all the work of Your hand.*

THE REAL MEANING OF PATIENCE

This is patience; knowing that God sees your big picture. He has written all of your chapters from beginning to end. Knowing whatever sufferings or problems you face, they are not without reason or without God.

◇ **God is in the midst of our problems.** ◇

I encourage you to be more like an eagle and be patient with the present. We should have confidence and know that the future holds possibilities that we may not be able to see.

> *Romans 12:12 KJV - Rejoicing in hope; patient in tribulation; continuing instant in prayer;*
>
> *Jeremiah 17:7 KJV - Blessed is the man that trusteth in the Lord, and whose hope the Lord is.*

Seek after patience. Learn how to let go, and wait on God to work it out. It does not mean we are to do nothing, no.

◊ **Trust in Him while He is doing His work.** ◊

Watch Him unwrap every layer of what He is doing. Your trust has to be in the Lord!

HIGH FLIERS

Eagles can fly high above storm clouds at around 10,000 to 15,000 feet in the sky. This behavior earned them the name of, "High Fliers." To be a, "High Flier," patience is required. They are waiting for the perfect moment to use the wind currents from the storm to ascend higher into the sky.

> *Romans 8:25 NKJV - But if we hope for what we do not see, we eagerly wait for [it] with perseverance.*

Eagles use wind turbulence to take them higher and higher into the sky. The turbulence relates to the trials that we face in this life. The Holy Spirit can use those things that were meant to bring us down, break us, or destroy us, and instead lift us up into His glorious presence where we can receive peace.

SPREAD YOUR WINGS AND SOAR

> *We get to a place where we can soar effortlessly by the power of the Holy Spirit.*

He will carry us when times get rough and when turmoil arises. He is our Comforter that shall never leave or forsake us. We can trust Him.

John 14:16 KJV - And I will pray the Father, and He shall give you another Comforter, that He may abide with you forever;

The gift of the Comforter is the great gift to the believer. It is by the power of the Holy Spirit that we are able to have the patience that is needed to be spiritual eagles. Through the Comforter, we will be able to please God in our walk and lifestyle.

2 Corinthians 12:9 AMP - but He has said to me, "My grace is sufficient for you [My lovingkindness and My mercy are more than enough—always available—regardless of the situation]; for [My] power is being perfected [and is completed and shows itself most effectively] in [your] weakness." Therefore, I will all the more gladly boast in my weaknesses, so that the power of Christ [may completely enfold me and] may dwell in me.

We all have struggles and challenges, but God wants us to fly above the storms.

**We have got to learn
to glide on the storm.**

Wait on the Lord. Be encouraged and He will strengthen your heart!

GOD'S WORD SAYS 

Psalms 37:7-9 ESV - 7 Be still before the Lord and wait patiently for Him; fret not yourself over the one who prospers in his way, over the man who carries out evil devices! 8 Refrain from anger, and forsake wrath! Fret not yourself; it tends only to evil. 9 For the evildoers shall be cut off, but those who wait for the Lord shall inherit the land.

Luke 21:19 KJV - In your patience possess ye your souls.

Our patience has much to do with how we relate to God.

Our patience is so vital.

You need patience even though He may know your heart; you have to learn to be patient and wait on the Lord. You need to learn how to put your confidence in Him.

Remember, patience is defined as the ability to tolerate delays, problems or sufferings without becoming anxious. No one wants to suffer or go through hard and difficult times, but in the midst of those times… God is trying to do something! Remember Job and all he went through? God revealed Himself strong in his life, and Job got double for all his trouble, because he waited on God.

2 Corinthians 6:4 KJV - But in all things approving ourselves as the ministers of God, in much patience, in afflictions, in necessities, in distresses,

We need to maintain our composure when in the thick of things, and know that beyond the shadow of a doubt that God has us! He is the One who is bringing us through all of this! Not everybody is going to have a Job situation, but we will all have our own cross to bear. Know that God is more than able to help in your situation, and He can bring out of you what He is desiring out of your life.

2 Corinthians 12:12 KJV - Truly the signs of an apostle were wrought among you in all patience, in signs, and wonders, and mighty deeds.

> **No matter the problems that we face, we need to be faithful to God.**

We must allow patience to have its perfect work in our lives. Get ready to fly on the storm!

> *Hebrews 12:1 NKJV - Therefore we also, since we are surrounded by so great a cloud of witnesses, let us lay aside every weight, and the sin which so easily ensnares [us], and let us run with endurance the race that is set before us,*

In our everyday walk with the Lord, we must stay focused. We cannot let Satan have his way. We continue to fight him with the Word and patiently wait on God. We will not allow the adversary to steal away our peace or our joy. We will not allow him to derail us from God's plans for our lives. We will continue to run with patience the race before us.

> *Romans 5:3-5 AMP - 3 And not only this, but [with joy] let us exult in our sufferings and rejoice in our hardships, knowing that hardship (distress, pressure, trouble) produces patient endurance; 4 and endurance, proven character (Spiritual maturity); and proven character, hope of a confident assurance [of eternal salvation]. 5 Such hope [in God's promises] never disappoints us, because God's love has been abundantly*

> *poured out within our hearts through the Holy Spirit who was given to us.*

You gain valuable experience as you go through trials.

Patience allows you to grow in God and mature in Him; you will not be a novice anymore.

As you let patience do its perfect work in you, you shall become the spiritual eagle that He is calling you to be. Your character in Christ will continue to increase and your spiritual maturity will cause you to draw closer to God. You will realize that no matter what happens, you already have an eternal deliverance!

We move forward through hardship and distress to obtain the just reward of our faith. God has blessings in store for us. We have to receive them in patience letting our hearts be fully persuaded of them.

We want instant, "microwave," results, but maturity takes time.

A home-cooked meal on the stove-top or in the oven always tastes better than a microwave dinner. The longer it takes, the more valuable and appreciated the final result will be. Anyone who endeavors to do something great in God's kingdom shall have to go through difficult things. To be victorious, you have to overcome something. It builds your faith up to trust God for greater and bigger things when you list all the victories He has brought you through.

> *James 1:3-4 AMP - 3 Be assured that the testing of your faith [through experience] produces endurance [leading to spiritual maturity, and inner peace]. 4 And let endurance have its perfect result and do a thorough work, so that you may be perfect and completely developed [in your faith], lacking in nothing.*

God's track record in your life is one of your greatest weapons against Satan.

**God wants your faith
to be complete in Him.**

The problems we face will force us to try our heart. Through the trying process, our faith is revealed. Once our faith is matured, we are able to produce great and glorious works for God.

EAGLES WAIT FOR THEIR PREY

Eagles know how to wait. They are vigilant to watch out for potential prey. Even if a rabbit goes into a hidey-hole, the eagle can outlast him. He will wait for hours until the rabbit comes back out. He will not miss the opportunity and will quickly grab that rabbit for dinner. The eagle's patience is rewarded. The eagle will not go hungry for the next several days because it waited.

We have to learn to put our faith and confidence in God.

> The more tests that we pass through victoriously, the more our confidence in God grows.

You will trust that God is able to take you through whatever stands in your way. Patience is needed, so we can mature and grow in God.

As I have served the Lord over these past fifty years, there have been many times that I have had to allow God to keep me settled as I fulfilled my assignment as pastor. There have been times that members have gotten offended because they felt like things should have been handled differently. But as a leader of God's people, I had to use patience in helping those that needed help along the way. Today, many of those individuals have grown into great spiritual eagles for God.

> **By our patience, we will see God's glory being revealed in the lives of those that come in our path.**

We live in a stressful world. There are so many attacks coming from every direction. We must trust God to help us obtain victory.

> **We need patience operating in our lives if we are going to be triumphant.**

We need patience and it is a good thing that we have it because it is one of the fruit of the Spirit. God knew we would need patience to fly through the tempests of life. God designed the eagle to fly above the storms.

> **God designed us to also rise above the trials and soar unto victory in Him.**

Ride the storm today through the power of the Holy

Ghost and glide to victory!

THREE WAYS TO PRACTICE PATIENCE

Just like the farmer has to wait on his crops to produce, so we, too, must wait on the Lord.

CIRCUMSTANCES

We live in a fallen world. Many things come at us that are out of our control. We have to trust our sovereign God. He knows what is coming up, and He knows how to get us out of bad situations. Romans 8:28, paraphrased, tells us that all things work together for good to those who love God and are the called according to God's purpose.

> **We are the called and chosen children of God.**

He will not forsake His precious children. Trust God will work out your situation and give Him the praise in advance!

James 5:7 NKJV - Therefore be patient, brethren, until the coming of the Lord. See [how] the farmer waits for the precious fruit of the earth, waiting patiently for it until it receives the early and latter rain.

Can we even talk about patience without mentioning Job? He is a standard for suffering patiently. His circumstances were grave. He lost his children, his wealth, and his health all in quick succession. That should be enough to take the wind out of most anyone's wings!

Job 1:13-19 ESV - 13 Now there was a day when his sons and daughters were eating and drinking wine in their oldest brother's house, 14 and there came a messenger to Job and said, "The oxen were plowing and the donkeys feeding beside them, 15 and the Sabeans fell upon them and took them and struck down the servants with the edge of the sword, and I alone have escaped to tell you." 16 While he was yet speaking, there came another and said, "The fire of God fell from heaven and burned up the sheep and the servants and consumed them, and I alone have escaped to tell you." 17 While he was yet speaking, there came another and said, "The Chaldeans formed three groups and made a raid on the camels and took them and struck down the servants with the edge of the sword, and I alone have escaped to tell you." 18 While he was yet speaking, there came another and said, "Your sons and daughters were eating and drinking wine in their oldest brother's house,

> *19 and behold, a great wind came across the wilderness and struck the four corners of the house, and it fell upon the young people, and they are dead, and I alone have escaped to tell you."*

Wow! Can you imagine how that must have been? He lost almost everything in the span of a day. Yet, he did not turn on God even a bit. He still trusted in Him. Many Christians today do not have the kind of wherewithal to still believe God when circumstances change for the worst like they did for Job.

> *Job 1:20-22 ESV - 20 Then Job arose and tore his robe and shaved his head and fell on the ground and worshiped. 21 And he said, "Naked I came from my mother's womb, and naked shall I return. The Lord gave, and the Lord has taken away; blessed be the name of the Lord." 22 In all this Job did not sin or charge God with wrong.*

Job was able to still worship God in the midst of his greatest trial. Job is the oldest book in our modern day Bible. The timeframe for the book was before Abraham. Job had no written promise or sealed covenant to stand on besides the one God made with Adam and Eve. He had the innate knowledge of God. It is also possible he learned from a descendant of Seth how to worship God. The amazing thing is that Job did not blame God for any of these things happening. He had a good idea of who God was. It is a good thing too, because it was not God who did all this, it was Satan.

Job 42: 1-6,10-13 ESV - 1 Then Job answered the Lord and said: 2 "I know that you can do all things, and that no purpose of yours can be thwarted. 3 'Who is this that hides counsel without knowledge?'Therefore I have uttered what I did not understand,   things too wonderful for me, which I did not know. 4 'Hear, and I will speak; I will question you, and you make it known to me.'5 I had heard of you by the hearing of the ear,   but now my eye sees you; 6 therefore I despise myself, and repent in dust and ashes." ... 10 And the Lord restored the fortunes of Job, when he had prayed for his friends. And the Lord gave Job twice as much as he had before. 12 And the Lord blessed the latter days of Job more than his beginning. And he had 14,000 sheep, 6,000 camels, 1,000 yoke of oxen, and 1,000 female donkeys. 13 He had also seven sons and three daughters.

There are many chapters listed of Job complaining, and his friends trying to comfort him, but really making matters worse. Then, God appears in a whirlwind and speaks thunderously. Job has no answer for God, and realizes that it is not for him to understand why these things happened for he is not the judge. He repents from his way of thinking; prays for his friends, as commanded by the Lord for misrepresenting Him; and then God blesses him with twice as much as he had before. Job patiently endured the worst of circumstances and was able to receive a double-blessing! We also will have times where we will have to endure patient suffering but know that God is going to get a blessing to you once the trial is over.

PEOPLE WE DEAL WITH THAT ARE UNCHANGEABLE

Difficult people can try the nerves like none other. We have to be patient with all people. There are those who will not agree with you. You have to understand, you are not everyone's cup of tea. There are people that will not get along with you no matter what you do. This can even be in your own family or at work! We have to have patience while we pray for God to work on their hearts. There are those who will try to purposely hurt us, emotionally and sometimes physically. We cannot lash out or give up on them. God still wants them to be saved.

Jesus was able to stay silent while He was mistreated, abused, tortured, and betrayed. He

SPREAD YOUR WINGS AND SOAR

did not raise a single complaint against any of the perpetrators. If we could operate in patience like Jesus, we would all be doing well! Let us pray for those who mean us harm, and believe that God, in due time, will draw them to Himself.

James 5:10 NKJV - My brethren, take the prophets, who spoke in the name of the Lord, as an example of suffering and patience.

The prophet Jeremiah confronted many people in his day. He was the Lord's mouthpiece. He was commanded to speak the Word of the Lord from a young age.

Jeremiah 1:4-8 NKJV - 4 Then the word of the LORD came to me, saying: 5 "Before I formed you in the womb I knew you; Before you were born I sanctified you; I ordained you a prophet to the nations." 6 Then said I: "Ah, Lord GOD! Behold, I cannot speak, for I [am] a youth." 7 But the LORD said to me: "Do not say, 'I [am] a youth,' For you shall go to all to whom I send you, And whatever I command you, you shall speak. 8 Do not be afraid of their faces, For I [am] with you to deliver you," says the LORD.

He was not able to convince a single person to listen. God told him ahead of time they would not hearken to his voice; but God is just and will warn His people before doing anything. Jeremiah is also known as the weeping prophet. For he saw so many terrible things coming up for Israel, and was powerless to convince the people to listen. He had to have patience to follow God even when they threw him in prison, attacked him, vilified him, and made his life miserable. But Jeremiah could not stop. He wanted to, but his passion for God was too immense to withhold.

Jeremiah 20:7-9 NKJV - 7 O LORD, You induced me, and I was persuaded; You are stronger than I, and have prevailed. I am in derision daily; Everyone mocks me. 8 For when I spoke, I cried out; I shouted, "Violence and plunder!" Because the word of the LORD was made to me A reproach and a derision daily. 9 Then I said, "I will not make mention of Him, Nor speak anymore in His name." But [His word] was in my heart like a burning fire Shut up in my bones; I was weary of holding [it] back, And I could not.

Jeremiah dealt with difficult people all his life. It was through his patience that he did see some of the prophecies fulfilled in his lifetime. He trusted God to protect him while he did the work. We also must be willing to be patient in our calling and carry on even if we suffer severe persecution and derision from others.

PATIENCE WAITING ON GOD

Maturation, again, takes time.

> Patience is the process of maturation; your faith is growing so that you can receive from God.

When you find a promise in God's Word and you are standing on it, do not let anything or anyone convince you that it will not manifest. You must have an unshakeable confidence that God is going to do His part. Enjoy the journey with God. Do not get hasty. He takes us through life in steps.

> Each step will lead to bigger and greater things.

Trust He is working on your heart. Give Him thanks for all the awesome things He has in store for you. Know that your God is working on your behalf to reveal His glory!

James 5:11 KJV - Behold, we count them happy which endure. Ye have heard of the patience of Job, and have seen the end of the Lord; that the Lord is very pitiful, and of tender mercy.

SPREAD YOUR WINGS AND SOAR

God chose Noah to be the one to bring salvation to mankind after the flood. He was a just and perfect man in his generation. God gave him an assignment that required him to fly alone. He had to trust God; for no one to that point had ever seen a flood.

> *Genesis 6:12-14 NKJV - 12 So God looked upon the earth, and indeed it was corrupt; for all flesh had corrupted their way on the earth. 13 And God said to Noah, "The end of all flesh has come before Me, for the earth is filled with violence through them; and behold, I will destroy them with the earth. 14 "Make yourself an ark of gopherwood; make rooms in the ark, and cover it inside and outside with pitch.*

Noah had to have a strong constitution within him to work diligently for 120 years preaching and building the ark. He worked faithfully without knowing the exact time that God would fulfill his judgment. He exhibited courage to stay the course until he heard God's voice.

> *Genesis 7:4-5 NKJV - 4 "For after seven more days I will cause it to rain on the earth forty days and forty nights, and I will destroy from the face of the earth all living things that I have made." 5 And Noah did according to all that the LORD commanded him.*

I see Noah as a spiritual eagle that performs his call without a fan club or cheerleaders to push him. He heard God's command and that was enough for him to be ready within seven days of when God was ready to bring the rain. We should follow his example and continue doing whatever God has asked us to do without complaint or support from others.

⧊   *We must be patient waiting on God.*   ⧊

SUMMARY

In summary, trust God in the process, under the pressure, and know He is working out all things out for your good! Sometimes it is our choices that get us in a mess, but many times we have been put in a place for a purpose and a reason. God will work all things out when we let Him. We need to have the same patience as the eagle that waits on their prey. Wait on God, wait on the storms, and rise above it. It is the same thing God is wanting from us in our lives. He is looking for us to believe Him, trust Him, and depend on Him!

Be like Job, and do not allow circumstances to affect your patience. Be like Jeremiah, and do what you have been commanded by God no matter what kind of persecution you will face. Be like Noah, and wait on God for the fulfillment of His Word no matter how long it takes; keep working and doing what you know to do. You will fly high above the storm, you patient, high-flying eagle.

PRAYER

Father God, I thank You and bless You. We thank You for giving us the patience that we need, and exactly when we need it! Help us to be patient when things do not go the way we think they should. Help us to be patient when others persecute us or attempt to harm us. Help us to be patient when we are not seeing the results of our faith immediately. Show us Your perspective far above the storms, so that we can soar to our victory in You. Holy Spirit, we ask that You do the work that needs to be done in our hearts, minds, and lives. God, we give You the praise, honor, and glory for doing it. In Jesus' name we pray. Amen.

SPREAD YOUR WINGS AND SOAR

Very Patient | Chapter 6

CHAPTER 7

NEST IN WILDERNESS

EAGLES LIKE THE WILDERNESS

Mother eagles prepare nests for their eaglets in the wilderness. They want to stay secluded from society that could bother them. This is done so she can raise them up without any outside interference. In comparison to us, God will raise His children in a secluded wilderness setting as well. It is a training ground of sorts.

Wilderness: an uncultivated, uninhabited, and inhospitable region. From that definition, I can understand why an eagle would build its nest there. She is protecting her babies from all the dangers of the outside world, and keeping herself and them from distractions that could take her attention away from them. The wilderness seems like a safe place for birthing and raising; if you are an eagle. But what if you were the Israelites wandering in the wilderness for all those years, unable to cross over into the land promised to you? What if you were David living in caves in the wilderness, hiding from an enemy who wants to kill you? Does it seem like such a great place to be in those circumstances?

WHAT IS THE WILDERNESS?

We have to understand that time is a process. We want what we want and want it immediately!

◇   **God allows time to be in the picture.**   ◇

But we need to understand our time in the wilderness - it is where we get our experience!

What does the wilderness mean to the Christian believer? The wilderness is the period of development and training while waiting on God's perfect timing. You may have committed your life to Christ many years ago, but it may be many more years before you reach the assignment that He has planned for your life. I have found myself in the wilderness on several occasions. It felt like the darkness and loneliness were never going to leave me. Strife and disharmony seemed to be taking over my being. Where do I go that He is not there? Who can I turn to for guidance and support? How can I get beyond this feeling of isolation in the wilderness of my own mind? I am not alone. I am never alone. Jesus is always with me, no matter where I am.

It is in the wilderness that I am at full attention, waiting for what my Lord will do next! I am waiting for how I can be used to bring glory to Him. It is in these times of waiting that I am most vulnerable, yet expectant of what God is doing. In these wilderness moments, I am most available for growth and change. In these times, we can choose growth, even if we feel afraid. Are you feeling like you are in your wilderness setting? Are you waiting on the Lord to reveal your calling?

**It is in the waiting
where we can find our strength!**

Isaiah 40:31 NKJV - But those who wait on the LORD Shall renew their strength. They shall mount up with wings like eagles. They shall run and not be weary, they shall walk and not faint.

PREPARATION IN THE WILDERNESS

The wilderness is a season for us to be trained, shaped, and molded into what God has designed us to be! It is not an overnight feeling for these things need to gradually take place for you to be equipped to do what God has called you to do! The wilderness is a good thing!

Little by little, you have to realize God is bringing you to the place of ultimate work for Him! Like Esther, we will be brought to a place for such a time as this.

> *Esther 4:14-16 ESV - 14 For if you keep silent at this time, relief and deliverance will rise for the Jews from another place, but you and your father's house will perish. And who knows whether you have not come to the kingdom for such a time as this?" 15 Then Esther told them to reply to Mordecai, 16 "Go, gather all the Jews to be found in Susa, and hold a fast on my behalf, and do not eat or drink for three days, night or day. I and my young women will also fast as you do. Then I will go to the king, though it is against the law, and if I perish, I perish."*

Esther was in a wilderness situation, but God had positioned her to save her people from the evil Haman. During her wilderness, she was being prepared to go on stage and represent God through her beauty. In verses 13 and 14, Mordecai tells her do not think you are going to escape or be silent at this time. For if you do not do it, God will raise up another.

Compared to the eagle, God has a divine calling on each of us, and we must realize that there is no way out.

> Eagles have to perform up
> to their instinctive abilities.

This is the same with you and I, as we serve God with our gifts and talents.

LIFE'S SEASONS

> You may not have foreseen your current
> circumstance, but God did.

God is not surprised. He is not disappointed. He does not need a Plan B. As unthinkable as it may seem, you are exactly where He has placed you.

Each of us, as we experience the wilderness of God, must consistently realize that God is trying to move you forward, trying to take you to a better place, and do greater things in your life!

> *Ecclesiastes 3:1 KJV - 1 To every thing there is a season, and a time to every purpose under the heaven:*

Solomon shared his wisdom by saying life is a series of seasons. While doing ministry for God, we will find ourselves in places that require us to trust God like never before. It is during these times that God displays His transforming power in our lives.

TO MOVE OR WAIT? FOLLOWING GOD'S PLAN

God knows the time and plan.

- Joseph waited 13 years
- Abraham waited 25 years
- Moses waited 40 years
- Jesus waited 30 years

If God is making you wait… you are in good company! Over my life, I have had to share in the waiting game. It seemed like there would never be a change to the test and trial that I was going through.

The more that I would wait, the more I would have to trust Him. But in every situation, God would always bring me through. God is still working on each of us, slowly but surely! We are becoming more equipped, far stronger, and increasingly powerful in Him to do more damage to the enemy.

JOSEPH – 13 YEARS

You can read in Genesis chapters 37 through 50, the story of Joseph. After telling his brothers the dreams he had, they wanted to put him in a pit at first and leave him for dead; but then they sold Joseph into slavery. He was bought by an Egyptian named Potiphar, from the Ishmaelites, who then made Joseph overseer over his house. Later, Joseph was unjustly accused by Potiphar's wife, and was imprisoned for 10 years.

Then we find, at 30 years of age, and after interpreting the Pharaoh's dream, he was released for his divine purpose! Why did he have to deal with these? God had a plan!

> Joseph became a bigger blessing by going through his wilderness period.

We may not always understand what we go through, but we can be reassured that God has a plan and a purpose for our lives.

MOSES - 40 YEARS

God had predestined this baby eaglet Moses to set His people free. Moses was trained in the palace of Pharaoh. God allowed this process as a training time in which he became familiar with the customs and practices of the Egyptians. Decades later after Moses failed, God called him, at the burning bush, for his assignment: in the midst of a literal wilderness.

> *Acts 7:29-30 KJV - 29 Then fled Moses at this saying, and was a stranger in the land of Midian, where he begat two sons. 30 And when forty years were expired, there appeared to him in the wilderness of mount Sinai an angel of the Lord in a flame of fire in a bush.*

Whether you have support or not, even if you do not see it, you have got to believe it! God has not forsaken you!

God is still working on you, shaping, and making you into what He designed you to be.

He is still concerned about bringing you to that place of divine calling!

Moses knew he was a Jew and missed his timing.

> **But we have to know God's timing and plan to accomplish His will in our lives.**

Moses missed the time and appointment. We cannot miss God's plan and timing; for if we do we will find ourselves in a very difficult place in our walk with God. God is able to reroute you, but it shall be a rougher ride than if you had waited for God's timing.

> *Genesis 15:13 NKJV - Then He said to Abram: "Know certainly that your descendants will be strangers in a land [that is] not theirs, and will serve them, and they will afflict them four hundred years.*
>
> *Exodus 12:40 KJV - Now the sojourning of the children of Israel, who dwelt in Egypt, was four hundred and thirty years.*

ABRAHAM 25 YEARS

God promised a son to Abraham.

> *Genesis 15:3-6 NKJV - 3 Then Abram said, "Look, You have given me no offspring; indeed one born in my house is my heir!" 4 And behold, the word of the LORD [came] to him, saying, "This one shall not be your heir, but one who will come*

> *from your own body shall be your heir." 5 Then He brought him outside and said, "Look now toward heaven, and count the stars if you are able to number them." And He said to him, "So shall your descendants be." 6 And he believed in the LORD, and He accounted it to him for righteousness.*

It took 25 years for the promise to be fulfilled. Abraham was traveling through the wilderness of the desert as the Lord led. He trusted in God during the wilderness. He realized there was no going back to his old country. He was set apart for God's use. He believed God and that was what made him righteous.

> *Genesis 21:5 KJV - And Abraham was a hundred years old, when his son Isaac was born unto him.*

The wilderness can lead us to a place of questioning who do we go to and where do we go? There is a perfect timing to God's plans. Sometimes we just need to wait where we are and let God do what He does. When God gives you a word, stand on it; for God is faithful to uphold His word.

JESUS 30 YEARS

> *Matthew 3:16-17 KJV - 16 And Jesus, when he was baptized, went up straightway out of the*

water: and, lo, the heavens were opened unto Him, and He saw the Spirit of God descending like a dove, and lighting upon Him: 17 And lo a voice from heaven, saying, This is My beloved Son, in whom I am well pleased.

Matthew 4:1-2 KJV - 1 Then was Jesus led up of the Spirit into the wilderness to be tempted of the devil. 2 And when He had fasted forty days and forty nights, He was afterward an hungered.

We as believers, will find that there will be times when God is going to call us to be in the wilderness experience for our development and growth.

The wilderness allows us to walk, talk, reflect, and connect to Him in a greater way.

It is for us to be brought to a better place with Him! God is leading you to the promised land [whatever He wants to bless you with]!

Mark 1:10-15 NKJV - 10 And immediately, coming up from the water, He saw the heavens parting and the Spirit descending upon Him like a dove. 11 Then a voice came from heaven, "You are My beloved Son, in whom I am well pleased." 12 Immediately the Spirit drove Him into the wilderness. 13 And He was there in the wilderness forty days, tempted by Satan,

> *and was with the wild beasts; and the angels ministered to Him. 14 Now after John was put in prison, Jesus came to Galilee, preaching the gospel of the kingdom of God, 15 and saying, "The time is fulfilled, and the kingdom of God is at hand. Repent, and believe in the gospel."*

Just like with Jesus as He was preparing for His earthly ministry, there are times in our lives we need to be prepared in the same way. There will be ugly and difficult periods, but all of it is for our betterment. God is equipping us so we can get to where He needs us to be.

WAITING ON GOD

We need to be joyful in the midst of our wait! Have peace and rejoice with a spirit of thanksgiving! We cannot be complaining. We have to learn to bless God in our wait. How can you be an eagle if you cannot be an eaglet? You must embrace the wilderness where eaglets grow into eagles.

God is watching and seeing! He is seeing whether He can depend on you. We need to realize that while we are waiting, we need to stay focused on Him! If you are faithful over a few things, He will make you lord over many. You cannot flip it around!

◇ **Let us wait on the Lord and be encouraged.** ◇

Be excited about waiting on God. He is preparing you for the work He has called you to!

WAITING ON OUR MINISTRY

We need time and maturity. God wants us to be prepared. He wants to shape and mold us to where He can be glorified in the best way.

My journey in ministry began as a teenager at my home church in Indianapolis. Working as a program planner, choir member, keyboard player, kitchen helper, and altar worker. At the age of 17, I would travel to different cities to assist small churches as a keyboardist.

In 1975, I was asked by Elder John Rolle to go to Brazil, IN. About 55 miles out of Indianapolis to assist him in ministry. I did not know what my calling was at that time, but I just wanted to be used by God. Well, it was during this wilderness experience that God used me to build a youth department of about 25 youth, start a gospel choir, assist with all the plans and permits for the new building that was built, and start the development of my construction skills that I use today. It was there that I began my preaching ministry alone with several other young preachers. After about 7 years, God moved me to another location to grow in Him.

SPREAD YOUR WINGS AND SOAR

Romans 12:5-8 NKJV - 5 so we, [being] many, are one body in Christ, and individually members of one another. 6 Having then gifts differing according to the grace that is given to us, [let us use them]: if prophecy, [let us prophesy] in proportion to our faith; 7 or ministry, [let us use it] in [our] ministering; he who teaches, in teaching; 8 he who exhorts, in exhortation; he who gives, with liberality; he who leads, with diligence; he who shows mercy, with cheerfulness.

It is a process. Lots of pressing must be done. But we have not seen the whole story yet! The plan of God with the timing of God will bring forth the blessing of God. We need to wait on the Lord!

NOT A NOVICE

1 Timothy 3:1-7 NKJV - 1 This [is] a faithful saying: If a man desires the position of a bishop, he desires a good work. 2 A bishop then must be blameless, the husband of one wife, temperate, sober-minded, of good behavior, hospitable, able to teach; 3 not given to wine, not violent, not greedy for money, but gentle, not quarrelsome, not covetous; 4 one who rules his own house well, having [his] children in submission with all reverence 5 (for if a man does not know how to rule his own house, how will he take care of the church of God?); 6 not a novice, lest being puffed up with pride he fall into the [same]

"

> *condemnation as the devil. 7 Moreover he must have a good testimony among those who are outside, lest he fall into reproach and the snare of the devil.*

Though this talks about a Bishop, this is for anyone that has been called into ministry. We must remain teachable and be able to learn from others.

We must trust in God's timing, so as to do the will of God and not be hasty.

There is a time to fly and His timing is perfect!

Everyone has an assignment.

Yes, each one of us, that God has called us to do!

SUMMARY

In summary, God uses the wilderness to prepare you for His use. Mother eagles build their nests in the wilderness to keep their eaglets away from distractions and interference that could be caused by society. God will do the same with us. He will place us into a time where we have to learn to trust Him. Only those who are completely surrendered to the Lord will be tried in this way.

Every single prophet, teacher, and apostle went

through a wilderness stage in their lives. Sometimes, you may go through multiple seasons of it, but allow it to build you up and not tear you down. Focus on the growth that you are obtaining in God. You are being shaped, molded, and formed into the perfect vessel to display God's greatness to the world. Keep your joy full and your praise turned up high. Be encouraged, that the wilderness is shaping you into what God desires you to be. Remain joyful, for you are being groomed into a victorious flier, you conquering eagle.

PRAYER

Father God, we give You all the glory and honor! Thank You for the time of preparation, so that we may be equipped to do the work You are calling us to do. Help shape and mold us into the people You created us to be. We know that the calling You have for us is going to exceed our imaginations. We trust You will be with us all the way. Give us the wisdom to wait on You and not miss your timing. We trust in Your promises. We know You are working out everything for our good. We thank You for loving us Father! In Your name Jesus, we pray. Amen.

CHAPTER 8

FAITHFUL FOR LIFE

FAITHFUL MATES

Male and female eagles stay together for life. They will raise their eaglets together. They sometimes hunt together. They will preen each other in an intimate time of showing the utmost care for each other's well-being. They will never forsake the other until death does them part.

> We need to be more like the eagle and remain faithful to God, our callings, and our spouses.

Let us take a look at what faithfulness is:
- Steadfast in affection; allegiance; a loyal and faithful friend.

- Firm in adherence to promises or in observance to duty: conscientious; a faithful employee, given with strong assurance; binding a faithful promise.

We need to emulate the fact that eagles are faithful for life. The definition of faithful is to be loyal, constant, and steadfast. In other words giving, showing firm, constant support, and demonstrating an allegiance that never falters.

Deuteronomy 31:6 KJV - Be strong and of a good courage, fear not, nor be afraid of them: for the Lord thy God, He it is that doth go with thee; He will not fail thee, nor forsake thee.

Hebrews 13:5 NKJV - [Let your] conduct [be] without covetousness; [be] content with such things as you have. For He Himself has said, "I will never leave you nor forsake you."

SECURE UNDER HIS WINGS

The psalmist expressed the faithfulness of the Lord in the fact that He will cover us with His feathers and allow us to be secure under His wings.

SPREAD YOUR WINGS AND SOAR

Psalm 91:4 KJV - He shall cover thee with His feathers, and under His wings shall thou trust: His truth shall be thy shield and buckler.

God gives power to the powerless. The youth will fall in exhaustion; but those who trust in the Lord, they will find new strength! They will soar high on wings like eagles. They will run and not grow weary. They will walk and not faint. We need to be those kinds of people.

Over and over again, God's Word reminds us that we are secure in Him and He will always be there. He is for us and with us always! We have this promise that He will be with us and that He will never leave us.

If God is going to be faithful to us, we need to be faithful to Him.

We need to learn how to be faithful to Him in our walk with Him.

Sometimes we are up, sometimes we are down, but we do not have to be that way with God. We can soar like an eagle! Because when that storm comes, the eagle just goes into it and glides on that storm! We can trust God because He has said that He will never leave us, nor forsake us!

You need to hear this, that when we hold fast to our faith, it helps us to be faithful.

> **It takes a lot of faith
> to step out in courage.**

Most people tend to resist change. We want to stay in our comfort zone, and it is usually not until the circumstances in our lives get rearranged that we not only find God is still with us; we also see His glory come out of every circumstance!

> *Joshua 1:9 KJV - Have not I commanded thee? Be strong and of a good courage; be not afraid, neither be thou dismayed: for the Lord thy God is with thee whithersoever thou goest.*

We can find a great example of God's faithfulness in the book of Ruth. The book of Ruth starts with a man and his wife Naomi, moving to Moab from Bethlehem because of a great famine in the land. The man and his wife had two sons. Due to unforeseen events, the husband died. The two sons also died and left two widows: Ruth and Orpah, who were from Moab. Naomi was distraught and wanted to return to her hometown; she had heard that God was providing bread for His people.

Naomi's widowed two daughter-in-laws,

Orpah and Ruth, wanted to travel with her, but Naomi insisted they stay in their land. Orpah returned, but Ruth resisted and continued on with Naomi. Because Naomi's life was a powerful witness to the reality of God, Ruth was drawn to her and the God she worshiped. Ruth's life demonstrates great faith because even after losing her husband, she still wanted to follow after her mother-in-law's God. What could she have seen in her mother-in-law's life, husband's life, that would make her want to trust in their God?

Ruth 1:15-18 NKJV - 15 And she said, "Look, your sister-in-law has gone back to her people and to her gods; return after your sister-in-law." 16 But Ruth said: "Entreat me not to leave you, [Or to] turn back from following after you; For wherever you go, I will go; And wherever you lodge, I will lodge; Your people [shall be] my people, And your God, my God. 17 Where you die, I will die, And there will I be buried. The LORD do so to me, and more also, If [anything but] death parts you and me." 18 When she saw that she was determined to go with her, she stopped speaking to her.

Ruth had found something better than anything in her own land. She saw how God worked in Naomi's life and learned how they worshiped

Him. She saw firsthand how her husband treated her with respect and love. She had a loving relationship with her mother-in-law. She could see the difference between the God of Israel and the Moab god of Chemosh. Even though she could have gone back home, she realized that nothing compared to the family she gained in Naomi and the loving God she was accustomed to.

Later on we see that God works mightily in Ruth's life. She honors her mother-in-law by following her advice and taking care of her. Ruth is a tireless worker and wants nothing more than to honor her mother-in-law and God above all else. What great faithfulness! The kinsman redeemer, Boaz, could not ignore such a humble and caring young woman.

Ruth 2:1-7 NKJV - 1 There was a relative of Naomi's husband, a man of great wealth, of the family of Elimelech. His name [was] Boaz. 2 So Ruth the Moabitess said to Naomi, "Please let me go to the field, and glean heads of grain after [him] in whose sight I may find favor." And she said to her, "Go, my daughter." 3 Then she left, and went and gleaned in the field after the reapers. And she happened to come to the part of the field [belonging] to Boaz, who [was] of the family of Elimelech. 4 Now behold, Boaz came from Bethlehem, and said to the reapers, "The LORD [be] with you!" And they answered him, "The LORD bless you!" 5 Then Boaz said to his servant

> who was in charge of the reapers, "Whose young woman [is] this?" 6 So the servant who was in charge of the reapers answered and said, "It [is] the young Moabite woman who came back with Naomi from the country of Moab. 7 "And she said, 'Please let me glean and gather after the reapers among the sheaves.' So she came and has continued from morning until now, though she rested a little in the house."

Boaz was attracted to this faithfulness. He saw that she cared about her mother-in-law. She worked long hours to gather enough for her mother-in-law to be provided for. She found grace (favor) in his sight because of her faithful work ethic to care for her mother-in-law.

> Ruth 2:8-10 NKJV - 8 Then Boaz said to Ruth, "You will listen, my daughter, will you not? Do not go to glean in another field, nor go from here, but stay close by my young women. 9 "[Let] your eyes [be] on the field which they reap, and go after them. Have I not commanded the young men not to touch you? And when you are thirsty, go to the vessels and drink from what the young men have drawn." 10 So she fell on her face, bowed down to the ground, and said to him, "Why have I found favor in your eyes, that you should take notice of me, since I [am] a foreigner?"

He immediately offers her protection. He tells

her not to go anywhere else. He commanded all the young men around her to not bother her. He also provides her with a source of water. This is absolute favor! She was not from Israel. She looked like a foreigner. She might have had an accent. She did not blend in and yet that did not stop her from doing what needed to be done. She was faithful to her mother-in-law. She humbled herself. I believe it was this humility that drew her late husband to marry her. Even as a stranger in a foreign land, she was able to find grace because she was faithful and humble.

Ruth 2:11-17 NKJV - 11 And Boaz answered and said to her, "It has been fully reported to me, all that you have done for your mother-in-law since the death of your husband, and [how] you have left your father and your mother and the land of your birth, and have come to a people whom you did not know before. 12 "The LORD repay your work, and a full reward be given you by the LORD God of Israel, under whose wings you have come for refuge." 13 Then she said, "Let me find favor in your sight, my lord; for you have comforted me, and have spoken kindly to your maidservant, though I am not like one of your maidservants." 14 Now Boaz said to her at mealtime, "Come here, and eat of the bread, and dip your piece of bread in the vinegar." So she sat beside the reapers, and he passed parched [grain] to her; and she ate and was satisfied, and kept some back. 15 And when she rose up to

> *glean, Boaz commanded his young men, saying, "Let her glean even among the sheaves, and do not reproach her. 16 "Also let [grain] from the bundles fall purposely for her; leave [it] that she may glean, and do not rebuke her." 17 So she gleaned in the field until evening, and beat out what she had gleaned, and it was about an ephah of barley.*

Boaz sees all that she is doing. He understands how hard it must have been for her to leave everything she knew and come to a land she knew nothing about. He recognizes that she truly wants to be here. He wants to help her and commands favor toward her. He feeds her with a nice meal to give her energy. He tells his people to let her glean from among the harvest and also to drop extra for her to pick up! Such favor! One of the most impactful Bible verses in all of Ruth is here in verse 12, "The LORD repay your work, and a full reward be given you by the LORD God of Israel, under whose wings you have come for refuge." This is a beautiful picture of God like a mother bird, sheltering her chicks from danger. It also speaks to the fact that the mother bird will provide for and take care of her chicks. Faithfulness!

Did Boaz know he was the kinsman's redeemer at this point? Had he already known that he was going to redeem her?

SPREAD YOUR WINGS AND SOAR

> **We do not know for sure, but we can see God's hand at work!**

She was able to bring home about 50 pounds of barley! It is uncommon for a gleaner to pull in that much. There was great favor upon her because of her faithfulness.

Ruth 2:18-20 NKJV - 18 Then she took [it] up and went into the city, and her mother-in-law saw what she had gleaned. So she brought out and gave to her what she had kept back after she had been satisfied. 19 And her mother-in-law said to her, "Where have you gleaned today? And where did you work? Blessed be the one who took notice of you." So she told her mother-in-law with whom she had worked, and said, "The man's name with whom I worked today [is] Boaz." 20 Then Naomi said to her daughter-in-law, "Blessed [be] he of the LORD, who has not forsaken His kindness to the living and the dead!" And Naomi said to her, "This man [is] a relation of ours, one of our close relatives."

When Noami saw the sheer amount of barley Ruth brought home, she knew that she had found grace in someone's sight. She wondered who it was and was excited to know that it was the kinsman redeemer! God had shown forth His favor in great measure. Noami realized there was a high probability to have her late husband's land redeemed by Boaz.

Throughout the rest of the book of Ruth, we see that the faithfulness of Ruth drew the blessing to her. Boaz, is a type and shadow of Jesus Christ. He greatly desired to redeem her life. In the same way, Jesus greatly desired to redeem us from sin's hold.

> **God honors faithfulness no matter race, creed, or culture.**

When He sees your faithfulness, then His faithfulness to bless, increase, multiply, provide, save, guide, and deliver is going to be shown. God is faithful to come through when you are being faithful to Him.

We can see God's impartiality in this precious story. Ruth belonged to another race that was despised by Israel. Moab had started fights and wars with Israel in the past which created bad blood between the nations. But God did not care about any of her past. He saw her faithfulness to Him. She could not help but be extremely blessed! She not only became a great-grandmother to King David but was a direct ancestor of Jesus! Do not let anyone disqualify you from serving God because of where and who you came from.

> **God can use anyone and every circumstance to build His kingdom!**

SPREAD YOUR WINGS AND SOAR

God is faithful to do great things in your life when you trust in Him!

> *Acts 10:34-35 KJV - 34 Then Peter opened his mouth, and said, Of a truth I perceive that God is no respecter of persons: 35 But in every nation he that feareth Him, and worketh righteousness, is accepted with Him.*

God is faithful in our lives even when we are not faithful. When we drop the ball, He is still faithful!

As spiritual eagles, God is calling us to be faithful to our assignments!

God is wanting us to have a mindset with a spirit of faithfulness to Him, one another, and our assignments.

An eagle mother is faithful to take care of her own. She knows exactly what they need and when they need it. Her eaglets do not have the capacity to understand what they truly need or desire. They are incapable of taking care of themselves. We are in the same boat. Only God can show us what we really need. We have to understand, we are incapable of taking care of ourselves! He knows what we need before we even ask Him!

◇ *We must rely on God in all things if we are* ◇
to survive and then thrive in this life.

He is trying to draw out the absolute best in our lives, and it starts with our faithfulness to Him.

> *Lamentations 3:22-23 KJV - 22 It is of the Lord's mercies that we are not consumed, because His compassions fail not. 23 They are new every morning: great is Thy faithfulness.*

FAITHFULNESS IS REWARDED

Being faithful will get you a lot more than trying to make a name for yourself. God will open doors and create opportunities because He honors faithfulness! God wants faithfulness.

◇ *Faithfulness is powerful and will get you into* ◇
places you cannot get into yourself!

In Hebrews chapter 11, we see the roll call of faith. These people, I call the pioneers of faith. It was their faith that they were commended for. They believed in who God was and what He was going to do. We can trust God in the same way; for He is faithful and our victories will be directly related to the role God wants us to play!

> Hebrews 11:1 KJV - Now faith is the substance of things hoped for, the evidence of things not seen.
>
> Hebrews 11:39-40 ESV - 39 And all these, though commended through their faith, did not receive what was promised, 40 since God had provided something better for us, that apart from us they should not be made perfect.

Glory be to God! Not only are we one in the body of Christ with all those alive, but we are also one with all those who ever lived! It takes all of us to be perfect in Him!

We must know that eagles are faithful to their abilities. They know what they can accomplish. They do not tackle things they are not meant to do. They understand their limitations. They are able to use their giftings to hunt, provide, and care for their young. They are faithful to do what they are called to do. In the same way, God has given us abilities to do things that He has called us to do. He needs us to be faithful to do those things that He has placed in us.

Let us look at what Jesus said about faithfulness. We are reading the parable of the talents. There are many ways to interpret this parable. I will be looking at the aspect of faithfulness to the gifts He has given us. Keep in mind that a talent is a weight of measurement. Depending on the place that set the scales, it could be anywhere between 58 pounds to 80 pounds. This is a huge sum of money in their time! What did the master expect them to do? Let us read.

> *Matthew 25:14-15 ESV - 14 "For it will be like a man going on a journey, who called his servants and entrusted to them his property. 15 To one he gave five talents, to another two, to another one, to each according to his ability. Then he went away.*

We can see that this boss man was vigilant. He was in-tune with his servants' abilities. He knew what they could handle. He trusted them to take care of His possessions.

We must know that God is in-tune with the abilities He gave us.

He trusts us to work in them for His kingdom. He knows just how we can use them to the best of our ability, and it is only through Him that they can be maximized.

SPREAD YOUR WINGS AND SOAR

Matthew 25:16 ESV - He who had received the five talents went at once and traded with them, and he made five talents more.

The one who had five talents immediately went to work. He doubled what was given to him. He was given five talents because his boss saw that he was capable. He believed that this servant was ready to work. This servant could have been in a waiting period for a while. It does not say how long the servants worked under their master. This man could have been watching and learning from his master for many years. He could have been advanced in age. He could have been the most faithful of servants and had the highest amount of trust in him. When the time came for him to step up and do like his master, he was ready. He was fully prepared to walk it out. His time for promotion had come. He was not going to let this opportunity escape him. We must also be fully prepared and ready to go as soon as the Lord asks us to. We hone our skills until they are ready to be used in a greater way.

Are you ready to be used?

God is looking for the willing and obedient; in other words: the faithful.

SPREAD YOUR WINGS AND SOAR

Matthew 25:17 ESV So also he who had the two talents made two talents more.

The second servant was able to double what was given to him. It does not say he went immediately to work, but when he did get going, he did well. He may not have been fully prepared to walk out and do what the master wanted, but he worked at it. He polished his abilities until they were able to bring forth fruit. We must always be working on the skills the Lord has given us. Excellence is what we should strive for.

Strive for excellence in everything that you do in life.

God will take you to the next level when He sees that you are ready and faithful.

Matthew 25:18 ESV - But he who had received the one talent went and dug in the ground and hid his master's money.

The servant with the one talent went and did nothing. He made no investments; he took no risks; he did not even attempt to step out and try anything. He decided in his mind, instead of possibly losing the money, that it would be better to hide it away and return it. This is the wrong way of thinking! Whatever is not growing is decreasing. Staying stuck means no forward progress is being made. Each day is an opportunity for us to grow. When we stay stuck, paralyzed by fear, we lose out on potential growth. We miss out on what God wants to do through us.

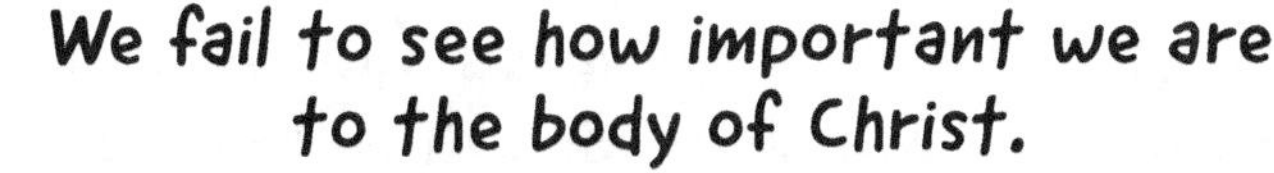

We fail to see how important we are to the body of Christ.

Each part must be working together to bring in a harvest for Jesus. When one of the parts is malfunctioning, it grinds the others to a halt. We must realize that God needs us to operate in our giftings. He needs each and every one of us. He would not have created us if there was no purpose. God saw the purpose ahead of time and then created you to fulfill it. We cannot allow fear to stop us from progressing in God. Be faithful to what God has given you.

Matthew 25:19-23 ESV - 19 Now after a long time the master of those servants came and settled accounts with them. 20 And he who had received the five talents came forward, bringing five talents more, saying, 'Master, you delivered to me five talents; here, I have made five talents more.' 21 His master said to him, 'Well done, good and faithful servant. You have been faithful over a little; I will set you over much. Enter into

> *the joy of your master.' 22 And he also who had the two talents came forward, saying, 'Master, you delivered to me two talents; here, I have made two talents more.' 23 His master said to him, 'Well done, good and faithful servant. You have been faithful over a little; I will set you over much. Enter into the joy of your master.'*

The master has come back and is checking on his servants. He wants to see what they have done with what he has given them. What does he find? The first two servants did well. They doubled what was given to them. They are called good and faithful. They are given more responsibility. They were able to enter into the joy of the Lord. They knew they had fulfilled their task. When God gives us things to do, and we are faithful to do them, He will reward us. He will promote us and move us into greater things. He is looking for those who are faithful with little. Faithfulness to God will take us further than trying to do it in our own power. The joy we shall experience will be unlike anything else. His joy will carry us along. Even when we feel like we have no strength; His joy becomes the motivating factor and persevering force that will propel us to do what He has commanded us to do.

> *Matthew 25:24-29 ESV - 24 He also who had received the one talent came forward, saying,*

SPREAD YOUR WINGS AND SOAR

> *'Master, I knew you to be a hard man, reaping where you did not sow, and gathering where you scattered no seed, 25 so I was afraid, and I went and hid your talent in the ground. Here, you have what is yours.' 26 But his master answered him, 'You wicked and slothful servant! You knew that I reap where I have not sown and gather where I scattered no seed? 27 Then you ought to have invested my money with the bankers, and at my coming I should have received what was my own with interest.*

Here come the excuses. The one with only one talent can only speak in fear. He was not willing to work. He was not willing to polish what had been given to him. He was not willing to step out in faith whatsoever. He was afraid, and admitted it to his master. I believe that this servant did not have a good image of their master. He may not have had a good relationship with him. It is so vitally important that we know who our God is. We need to understand His character and nature; for we will not trust or have faith in someone we do not know. We must believe that He is exactly as His Word describes. Faith works by love. If we do not receive the love of God, then we will have no faith to trust Him.

> *Galatians 5:6 AMP - For [if we are] in Christ Jesus neither circumcision nor uncircumcision means*

> *anything, but only faith activated and expressed and working through love.*

You can know God as much as you want. Scripture is rich and full of revelation.

The more you understand about God, the more you will trust Him.

That trust will allow faith to operate in you. That faith extended over long periods of time is faithfulness. You will want to carry out the tasks He has given you, because you have seen His goodness in your life, and you know that He is trying to bless another through you. Be faithful to God because He loves you, and it is your reasonable service or the absolute least you could do for Him. Without faith, it is impossible to please Him. I want to be a pleasing sacrifice to the Lord! What about you?

> *Matthew 25:28-29 ESV - 28 So take the talent from him and give it to him who has the ten talents. 29 For to everyone who has will more be given, and he will have an abundance. But from the one who has not, even what he has will be taken away.*

This can be hard to understand. Why would the one with the most be given even more? How is that fair? God is saying that those who are faithful in great measures will be counted worthy of even more responsibility. The ones with more will be given more because it has been proven to God that they are trustworthy. They will do what He has asked without question, without complaints, and without arguing.

I do not know about you, but I want to be one of those servants that is given more because God has seen my faithfulness in the small things! How about you? Are you wanting God to bless you with more? Are you wanting to see Him take you to places beyond what you can imagine? It starts with faithfulness in the little. Be faithful with what He has given you. Polish your gifts. Use the gifts He has given you. Be faithful in your everyday responsibilities. Do not allow fear to strangle your destiny.

> Once God sees you are ready, then be prepared to ascend into new territory on the wind of the Holy Spirit.

STAY FAITHFUL IN MARRIAGE

Eagles are faithful for life. Once eagles mate

with their significant others, they will never forsake them. They will always be there for each other. They will raise their children together and take care of each other when breeding season comes. In like manner, once God connects us to the person that He wants us to wed, then He will require us to stay loyal to them forever. Only death can break the covenant of marriage. In this day and age, the majority of marriages end in divorce.

> We need to prioritize and demonstrate faithfulness to our spouses to show the world how a marriage should be.

God abhors adultery! There are serious problems that will occur in each person's life who does not quickly turn away from this reprehensible behavior. Husbands and wives should honor the vows and commitments they promised to each other at the wedding altar. Marriage is serious business that God does not take lightly.

Not every day is going to be a walk in the park. You will have arguments with your spouse. You will fail to meet their expectations. You will disappoint them. However, the Holy Spirit will help us. Quickly forgive and forget with His guidance. Only Jesus was able to live perfectly. Husbands and wives are works-in-progress. Rely on God to help navigate your marriage. When He is at the center of it, it will be a blessing to you both.

Marriage is so rare today due to the many attacks from the enemy on families, the false definitions that are being applied to marriage, and the seed of sin that has pervaded to corrupt the holy union.

When two come together, it is God's intent for them to stay together for life.

That is His desire. No stone throwing here for God loves us all, but we need to get this into the young people: commitment!

As a young Christian, I learned the importance of marriage. I had the opportunity to sit in the Brotherhood Meetings and learn what God's Word spoke about marriage. Because I wanted to live my life in obedience to God's Word, I asked my high school sweetheart (Sarion Williams) to marry me at the age of 18. It has been because of the Lord's grace that we have been walking together now for 49 years. I praise God for

a God-fearing, gifted, and anointed woman of God that desires to please the Lord more than please me. When we seek to please the Lord, then we will treat each other the way that God desires us to.

Throughout these years, we have had many ups and downs, but through it all, God has been faithful to us. Lady Sarion, as she is fondly called, has stood by my side in every ministry that we have attended, and served faithfully as mother to our four children, ten grandchildren, and two great-grandchildren. She has served as First Lady in the Absolute Worship family for nearly 35 years. Glory to God for His keeping power in our lives!

People need to understand, before taking vows, that they need to be in the house of the Lord and be surrounded by like-minded believers. They should have some sort of pre-marital counseling to prepare them for their new life together. They need to look upon other older established Christian marriages and learn by example. They also need to learn how to take care of each other. This world is not going to help them here. Only the Word of God can do it! We need God's help!

Genesis 2:24 KJV - Therefore shall a man leave his father and his mother, and shall cleave unto his wife: and they shall be one flesh.

> *Mark 10:6-9 NKJV - 6 "But from the beginning of the creation, God 'made them male and female.' 7 'For this reason a man shall leave his father and mother and be joined to his wife, 8 'and the two shall become one flesh'; so then they are no longer two, but one flesh. 9 "Therefore what God has joined together, let not man separate."*

Those of you that are married, God is calling you to stay together. Those who are wanting to get married, should go into it with the mindset that you are going to stay in it! There is a mode of transportation here in Indianapolis that is called the Red Line. You get tickets to transfer to get off and on. That is not

God's desire for marriage!

> *He wants us to go into marriage with the mindset that we are going to be faithful to one another for life.*

Things do happen and issues can come up where others could not stay with that mate, but the bottom line is that we should want to stay together in the name of the Lord.

SUMMARY

In summary, male and female eagles are faithful to one another for life. We need to follow their example. We cannot afford to be up and down. God is wanting us to be faithful to Him like we learned from Ruth. God desires us to be faithful to our spouses just like Jesus is faithful to His church. God wants to bless us for being faithful to our responsibilities and our relationships. The Lord is coming back for a bride that has prepared herself!

Luke 12:35-39 NKJV - 35 "Let your waist be girded and [your] lamps burning; 36 "and you yourselves be like men who wait for their master, when he will return from the wedding, that when he comes and knocks they may open to him immediately. 37 "Blessed [are] those servants whom the master, when he comes, will find watching. Assuredly, I say to you that he will gird himself and have them sit down [to eat], and will come and serve them. 38 "And if he should come in the second watch, or come in the third watch, and find [them] so, blessed are those servants. 39 "But know this, that if the master of the house had known what hour the thief would come, he would have watched and not allowed his house to be broken into.

Journey on, you faithful eagle.

PRAYER

Father God, we give You all the honor and glory. Thank You for Your faithfulness. Help us to be faithful in all things! Remind us to look at the eagle and remember the faithfulness they show to their significant others. Give us the strength to remain faithful to our callings and responsibilities that You have given us. We trust in You and put our faith in You. We believe You will never let us down. We choose to be faithful to You in everything that we do in this life. In Your mighty name we pray Jesus. Amen!

CHAPTER 9

FLY ALONE

YOU ARE NEVER ALONE

Eagles are solitary birds. You will not find a bunch of eagles congregating. They do not flock together with others. They normally live in the same territory their entire lives. If there is a lack of food or water, they may migrate elsewhere. In comparison to us, there will be times in our lives, as believers, where we will have to fly alone; where the people around you cannot help you, and when the only One you can trust is God. The main thing you have to remember is that even if you feel alone… you are never alone!

Joshua 1:5 KJV - There shall not any man be able to stand before thee all the days of thy life: as I was with Moses, [so] I will be with thee: I will not fail thee, nor forsake thee.

CHOSEN - NOT JUST CALLED

The only way we are able to navigate alone as eagles is by God's Spirit; there is no other way. We all have room to do bigger and greater things in God. We all have a gift; we are to be busy using that gift for the Lord. We have all been given a calling from God. We have an assignment; a place in which we are called to work.

> **Many people have been given a calling, but few have chosen to walk it out.**

We have a responsibility to obey what God has asked us to do. We have to take ownership of our relationship with God to allow ourselves to be used of God, so that He gets all the glory. We do not want to just be called; we want to be chosen.

In the parable in Matthew 22:1-14 KJV - 14 For many are called, but few [are] chosen. This example showed that God is calling us to come to his Marriage supper (Relationship with Christ), but many are not willing to accept God's invitation. So because of their choice, they will not have a relationship with God.

YOU HAVE AN ASSIGNMENT

Everyone of us is important (valuable) to God. We all have an assignment we have to do alone. We would like to have support; we would like to have someone pushing us or someone patting us on the back. However, there are times that you will have to walk alone; seemingly, like no one else is on your side. We have to know though, we are all special. We have unique assignments in the Kingdom of God that only we can do; you were created for that job, and no one else has. Read the below scripture to get an idea of what Paul is telling us.

1 Corinthians 12:17-31 CEV - 17 If our bodies were only an eye, we couldn't hear a thing. And if they were only an ear, we couldn't smell a thing. 18 But God has put all parts of our body together in the way that he decided is best. 19 A body isn't really a body, unless there is more than one part. 20 It takes many parts to make a single body. 21 That's why the eyes cannot say they don't need the hands. That's also why the head cannot say it doesn't need the feet. 22 In fact, we cannot get along without the parts of the body that seem to be the weakest. 23 We take special care to dress up some parts of our bodies. We are modest about our personal parts,

24 but we don't have to be modest about other parts. God put our bodies together in such a way that even the parts that seem the least important are valuable. 25 He did this to make all parts of the body work together smoothly, with each part caring about the others. 26 If one part of our body hurts, we hurt all over. If one part of our body is honored, the whole body will be happy. 27 Together you are the body of Christ. Each one of you is part of his body. 28 First, God chose some people to be apostles and prophets and teachers for the church. But he also chose some to work miracles or heal the sick or help others or be leaders or speak different kinds of languages. 29 Not everyone is an apostle. Not everyone is a prophet. Not everyone is a teacher. Not everyone can work miracles. 30 Not everyone can heal the sick. Not everyone can speak different kinds of languages. Not everyone can tell what these languages mean. 31 I want you to desire the best gifts. So I will show you a much better way.

We are one body in Christ. His body has many members. Every joint should supply. Every part must be in working order. The parts must function for what they were created for. An eye cannot be an ear. An ear cannot be a mouth. A mouth cannot be a hand. Every part is distinct for its purpose. We must know that our gifts are important to God. He has placed us in His body for a specific reason and purpose. Your gifts and talents can only function to their highest capacity when used in alignment with God's divine plan.

FOLLOW GOD EVEN IF NO ONE ELSE DOES

Teenagers like to do things in droves. They call it peer-pressure for a reason. Everyone else is doing it so they feel left out if they do not. God will have you do what might be considered the unpopular thing. You will suffer hardship for following Jesus. You will lose relationships and friendships, but we are called to fly alone. If no one else follows the Lord or even agrees with you, then that should not affect your decision to follow God. You may not have the support of everyone around you. You will have to do some things alone.

Flying alone will get you to the destination that God wants you to be.

COMPLEMENTARY HELP

In specific seasons, we might have help. There are times where our goals will overlap with others. Look at Aaron and Moses.

SPREAD YOUR WINGS AND SOAR

> *Exodus 4:14-15 NKJV - 14 So the anger of the LORD was kindled against Moses, and He said: "Is not Aaron the Levite your brother? I know that he can speak well. And look, he is also coming out to meet you. When he sees you, he will be glad in his heart. 15 "Now you shall speak to him and put the words in his mouth. And I will be with your mouth and with his mouth, and I will teach you what you shall do.*

Moses was tending Jethro's sheep. He was learning to be a shepherd. Moses claimed he had a slow tongue or speech impediment that made talking difficult. After hearing Moses say this, God gives him Aaron to speak for him. There may be times where God hooks you up with another to fulfill the calling on your life. Praise the Lord when that happens! It is a wonderful thing to unite with fellow believers and make some things happen in God's kingdom! However, this could just be for a season.

Here is another example. This time another person was brought in for support. Look at Aaron and Hur with Moses.

> *Exodus 17:12 KJV - But Moses' hands were heavy; and they took a stone, and put it under him, and he sat thereon; and Aaron and Hur stayed up his hands, the one on the one side, and the other on the other side; and his hands were steady until the going down of the sun.*

Moses needed help. When his hands were up, the Israelites were winning. When they were down, they were losing. He was getting weary of keeping those hands held high. He had his brother and brother-in-law help him. They held up his hands so he could rest on the rock. This is an example of complementary help. He could not have accomplished this task without his family. We will not always have that kind of support. We have to learn to press on and persevere whether or not we have any sort of support or help on our side.

God is on your side.

Fly on eagle.

RECOGNIZE THE SEASONS

We have to recognize the opportunities around us. We need to be ready to fly solo. Look what Ecclesiastes tells us about seasons.

Ecclesiastes 3:1-8 CEV - 1 Everything on earth has its own time and its own season. 2 There is a time for birth and death, planting and reaping, 3 for killing and healing, destroying and building, 4 for crying and laughing, weeping and dancing,

> *5 for throwing stones and gathering stones, embracing and parting. 6 There is a time for finding and losing, keeping and giving, 7 for tearing and sewing, listening and speaking. 8 There is also a time for love and hate, for war and peace.*

We must learn when the right wind thermal of the Holy Spirit is coming by so you can fly on it to do what God has called you to do alone. Often, you feel alone in your calling.

When you have God on your side, it does not matter what it looks like.

It does not matter what things seem like. It does not matter how many you have on your side or against you; God is more than enough.

DAVID AND GOLIATH

Let us look at the life of David. He was a shepherd boy; the youngest of his family. The runt of the litter, so to speak. How was this little guy able to defeat a giant soldier like Goliath? Read on.

> *1 Samuel 17:26 KJV - And David spake to the men that stood by him, saying, What shall be done to the man that killeth this Philistine, and*

taketh away the reproach from Israel? for who is this uncircumcised Philistine, that he should defy the armies of the living God?

David was not a soldier; however, he did trust in God. He had been through some dire situations: killing both the lion and the bear with his own hands. That is some serious bravery, even for an adult!

1 Samuel 17:33-36 NKJV - 33 And Saul said to David, "You are not able to go against this Philistine to fight with him; for you [are] a youth, and he a man of war from his youth." 34 But David said to Saul, "Your servant used to keep his father's sheep, and when a lion or a bear came and took a lamb out of the flock, 35 "I went out after it and struck it, and delivered [the lamb] from its mouth; and when it arose against me, I caught [it] by its beard, and struck and killed it. 36 "Your servant has killed both lion and bear; and this uncircumcised Philistine will be like one of them, seeing he has defied the armies of the living God."

Due to the previous battles that David fought alone, it gave him the courage to challenge Goliath. The anointing on David's life was activated by his unwavering trust in God. His trust was built up during those times when he had to rely on God. There was no one else he could turn to. He could not defeat

Goliath without knowing that His God would back him up.

> **There will be times where only God is the One who is backing you up and that is okay.**

He is more than enough to defeat your enemies and get you where you need to go. David knew this very well. We know the story. David was able to convince Saul that he could fight Goliath. He used his sling and felled Goliath, and the army of the Philistines was routed by the Israelites. God made a name for David on that day, and it was because he followed Him alone.

DAVID AND SAUL

Here is another example from David's life. He felt isolated when Saul attempted to hunt him down. He escaped to the cave Adullam, and was there for a while.

1 Samuel 22:1 NKJV - David therefore departed from there and escaped to the cave of Adullam. So when his brothers and all his father's house heard [it], they went down there to him.

Everywhere David went, Saul went too. This had to have been an emotionally-draining experience for David. You can see it in his psalms. Look how he cries out to the Lord because he felt so alone.

Psalm 13:1-3 NKJV - 1 To the Chief Musician. A Psalm of David. How long, O LORD? Will You forget me forever? How long will You hide Your face from me? 2 How long shall I take counsel in my soul, [Having] sorrow in my heart daily? How long will my enemy be exalted over me? 3 Consider [and] hear me, O LORD my God; Enlighten my eyes, Lest I sleep the [sleep of] death;

We will have moments of loneliness; where it feels like no one cares or wants to help. During those times, we have to draw close to the Lord. He will be our Help and Strong Tower. We trust in Him and go it alone; even if the entire world is against us.

Psalms 61:3 KJV - For Thou hast been a shelter for me, and a strong tower from the enemy.

PETER AND JESUS

Let us not forget about Peter. He was one of Jesus' closest disciples. He followed Him devoutly. When Peter saw Jesus on the water and knew it was Him, he got the crazy idea that he could walk to Him. Now, how did Peter think he could walk on water?

What made him trust in Jesus so much that he could defy the laws of physics? Let us read and see.

> *Matthew 14:28-31 NKJV - 28 And Peter answered Him and said, "Lord, if it is You, command me to come to You on the water." 29 So He said, "Come." And when Peter had come down out of the boat, he walked on the water to go to Jesus. 30 But when he saw that the wind [was] boisterous, he was afraid; and beginning to sink he cried out, saying, "Lord, save me!" 31 And immediately Jesus stretched out [His] hand and caught him, and said to him, "O you of little faith, why did you doubt?"*

Peter was walking on the water! He was doing it. When his focus was on Jesus, he was fine. No one went with him. He had to walk alone. We also have times when we have to walk alone on the water toward Jesus. We cannot get distracted by circumstances or our environment. We cannot allow fear to stop us from pursuing Jesus.

⬦ Walk on, even if it must be alone. ⬦

Peter could have walked all the way to Jesus if he did not doubt. We must be fully persuaded that God will not let us drown. If we doubt Him, then we will sink. He can rescue us, but it is better to walk on the water alone. Though none go with us, still we will follow Him.

LEARN TO WORK ALONE 

We have to learn to work alone. We all have personal assignments from God that only we are able to do.

He will give you the wisdom to do it; but you have to trust Him.

Enjoy your alone time with God. That is how you will build a strong relationship with Him that will be able to last through any type of trouble.

HIGH PRIEST

Another example of doing the work alone is that of the High Priest: who would enter into the Holy of Holies on the Day of Atonement alone. There were many requirements that he had to follow; if he did not do it right: he would die. The High Priest had to go it alone. No one could help them.

Leviticus 16:2-6 NKJV - 2 and the LORD said to Moses: "Tell Aaron your brother not to come at [just] any time into the Holy [Place] inside the veil, before the mercy seat which [is] on the ark, lest he die; for I will appear in the cloud above the mercy seat. 3 "Thus Aaron shall come into the Holy [Place]: with [the blood of] a young bull as a sin offering, and [of] a ram as a burnt offering. 4 "He shall put the holy linen tunic and the linen trousers on his body; he shall be girded with a linen sash, and with the linen turban he shall be attired. These [are] holy garments. Therefore he shall wash his body in water, and put them on. 5 "And he shall take from the congregation of the children of Israel two kids of the goats as a sin offering, and one ram as a burnt offering. 6 "Aaron shall offer the bull as a sin offering, which [is] for himself, and make atonement for himself and for his house.

CORNELIUS

We can also look at Cornelius. He and his family alone were serving God. There was no one else around who cared. They had no support from a church or anything. He was a Gentile. He enjoyed giving alms to the poor and praying to God. He realized something was missing in his life. He had no church or assembly to learn from. God heard his prayers and sent Peter to bless him with what he needed.

Acts 10:1-6 NKJV - 1 There was a certain man in Caesarea called Cornelius, a centurion of what was called the Italian Regiment, 2 a devout [man] and one who feared God with all his household,

> *who gave alms generously to the people, and prayed to God always. 3 About the ninth hour of the day he saw clearly in a vision an angel of God coming in and saying to him, "Cornelius!" 4 And when he observed him, he was afraid, and said, "What is it, lord?" So he said to him, "Your prayers and your alms have come up for a memorial before God. 5 "Now send men to Joppa, and send for Simon whose surname is Peter. 6 "He is lodging with Simon, a tanner, whose house is by the sea. He will tell you what you must do."*

You must know that God sees you. He sees your faithfulness. Your faithfulness attracts the blessing of God to you. God will send you what you need as you remain faithful to follow Him; alone if you must. As a result of his prayers God filled him and his family with the baptism of the Holy Spirit and they were all baptized in the name of the Lord.

TABITHA

Who can forget about Tabitha (Dorcas)? She was a modern-day Mother Theresa. She served the poor with her sewing and gifts to the needy. A real Proverbs 31 woman. She was making a great impact in the Kingdom of God until a sickness took her down. Some of the disciples heard that Peter was not far, and they called for him to see her. He raised her from the dead, and it was a great sign to the village! On that day, many trusted in Jesus from that point forward.

> *Acts 9:36, 40-42 NKJV - 36 At Joppa there was a certain disciple named Tabitha, which is translated Dorcas. This woman was full of good works and charitable deeds which she did. ... 40 But Peter put them all out, and knelt down and prayed. And turning to the body he said, "Tabitha, arise." And she opened her eyes, and when she saw Peter she sat up. 41 Then he gave her [his] hand and lifted her up; and when he had called the saints and widows, he presented her alive. 42 And it became known throughout all Joppa, and many believed on the Lord.*

We serve the God of the resurrection. He can raise dead things to life. He can breathe new life into any dead situation. You may be called to raise the dead, and when that happens, most likely you will do it alone. You might be the only one around who believes that God can raise the dead. Do not let it affect you.

Do what needs to be done in the name of the Lord.

YOU WILL FEEL ALONE AT TIMES

Times of total isolation and feeling alone will come upon you. Know that you are not the first one who has ever felt this way. There are many people in the Bible who felt alone. Some felt like they were struggling, others were lonely, some were isolated, and many felt like nobody cared about them. You must know that God has not turned His back on you! He has not forsaken you!

⸎ **You have to learn to fly alone like an eagle.** ⸎

DAVID:

Psalms 38:4 KJV - For mine iniquities are gone over mine head: as an heavy burden they are too heavy for me.

Psalm 42:11 NKJV - Why are you cast down, O my soul? And why are you disquieted within me? Hope in God; For I shall yet praise Him, The help of my countenance and my God.

ELIJAH:

1 Kings 19:4 KJV - But he himself went a day's journey into the wilderness, and came and sat down under a juniper tree: and he requested for himself that he might die; and said, It is enough; now, O LORD, take away my life; for I am not better than my fathers.

JONAH:

Jonah 4:3 KJV - Therefore now, O LORD, take, I beseech thee, my life from me; for it is better for me to die than to live.

JOB:

Job 3:11,26 KJV - 11 Why died I not from the womb? why did I not give up the ghost when I came out of the belly? ... 26 I was not in safety, neither had I rest, neither was I quiet; yet trouble came.

Job 10:1 KJV - My soul is weary of my life; I will leave my complaint upon myself; I will speak in the bitterness of my soul.

MOSES:

Exodus 32:32 KJV - Yet now, if thou wilt forgive their sin--; and if not, blot me, I pray thee, out of thy book which thou hast written.

SPREAD YOUR WINGS AND SOAR

JEREMIAH:

Jeremiah 20:14,18 KJV - 14 Cursed be the day wherein I was born: let not the day wherein my mother bare me be blessed. 18 Wherefore came I forth out of the womb to see labor and sorrow, that my days should be consumed with shame?

JESUS:

Isaiah 53:3 KJV - He is despised and rejected of men; a man of sorrows, and acquainted with grief: and we hid as it were our faces from Him; He was despised, and we esteemed Him not.

Mark 14:34-36 KJV - 34 And saith unto them, My soul is exceeding sorrowful unto death: tarry ye here, and watch. 35 And He went forward a little, and fell on the ground, and prayed that, if it were possible, the hour might pass from him. 36 And He said, Abba, Father, all things are possible unto thee; take away this cup from me: nevertheless not what I will, but what Thou wilt.

Luke 22:44 KJV - And being in an agony He prayed more earnestly: and His sweat was as it were great drops of blood falling down to the ground.

SITUATIONS THAT MAKE YOU FEEL ALONE 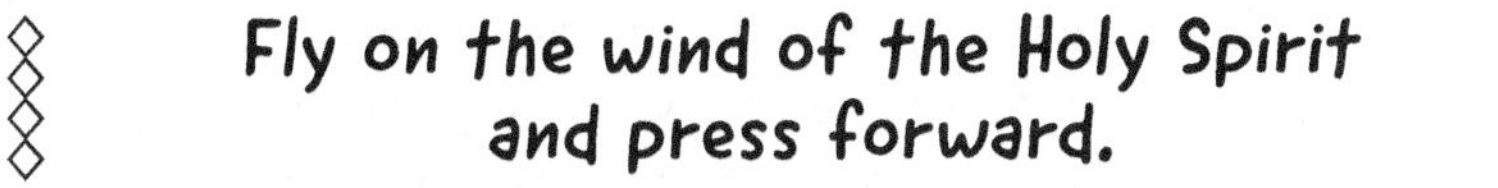

There are different situations in life that make you feel alone. However, you must leave the perch! Do not stay stuck where you are.

Fly on the wind of the Holy Spirit and press forward.

Below, I have listed some of the situations and reasons why people feel alone. Know that none of these things can hold you down because you are an eagle!

SICKNESS OR DISEASE

You feel:

- Your freedom is being taken away
- You are not able to do the things you used to
- You are the only one suffering and no one feels like you

Solution:

Jesus has provided healing for you. Read the following verse and believe it. You can be free today! Know that it can take time for physical things to be healed but do not lose heart.

Continue trusting God and
speaking forth His Word.

Isaiah 53:4-5 NKJV - 4 Surely He has borne our griefs And carried our sorrows; Yet we esteemed Him stricken, Smitten by God, and afflicted. 5 But He [was] wounded for our transgressions, [He was] bruised for our iniquities; The chastisement for our peace [was] upon Him, And by His stripes we are healed.

DEATH OF A LOVED ONE

You feel:

- You cannot continue life without them
- You long to be with them
- Life is incomplete without them

Solution:

Death is a foreign concept to eternal beings like us who were made to live forever. If the loved one has accepted Christ, then you will see them again. We can never be sure what people's final moments are like. When we get to Heaven, I believe we will be surprised by how many we thought were going the other direction that will be welcoming our arrival.

Hold fast to the hope that you truly do not know someone's eternal destination.

> *1 Thessalonians 4:13-14 KJV - 13 But I would not have you to be ignorant, brethren, concerning them which are asleep, that ye sorrow not, even as others which have no hope. 14 For if we believe that Jesus died and rose again, even so them also which sleep in Jesus will God bring with Him.*

TESTS AND TRIALS

You feel:

- No one cares about you
- Everyone is against you
- Co-workers do not like you
- Family causes drama for you
- Friends will betray you

Solution:

Jesus told us that we would suffer persecution. We cannot be surprised when it comes our way! We will have issues in the world just because we follow Jesus. We, however, do not need to worry, for He is our Overcomer.

*No matter what happens around us,
we know that victory is ours.*

John 16:33 KJV - These things I have spoken unto you, that in Me ye might have peace. In the world ye shall have tribulation: but be of good cheer; I have overcome the world.

FINANCIAL HARDSHIP

You feel:

- Inadequate, ashamed, and less than
- That you are trapped in debt and not able to get out of it
- God has let you down

Solution:

God is Your Source!

If you are having trouble then you need to understand that money is not your god. Money is a tool used to further the Kingdom of God on Earth and to take care of your needs. When you have the right concept of money, then you find it is easy to trust God for it. If you are afraid to give, then you have money on too high of a pedestal. Ask God for wisdom, for He is the one who gives you the ability to make money.

> *Deuteronomy 8:18 KJV - But thou shalt remember the LORD thy God: for it is He that giveth thee power to get wealth, that He may establish His covenant which He sware unto thy fathers, as it is this day.*

CHURCH HURT

You feel:

- You have not been treated well
- Betrayed or otherwise insignificant
- You cannot trust anyone, especially those in the church, which hurts your relationship with God

Solution:

Forgive and forget. People are flawed beings.

The only perfect human was Jesus; everyone else has work to do.

Know that people will offend you, but you do not have to receive the offense. You can let it slide right off you. Do not take up your own defense. Do not argue. Do not try to have your way. Forgive the offending party and move on. You may not trust that individual/organization the same way again, but it does not have to affect your relationship with God.

> *Matthew 18:21-22 NKJV - 21 Then Peter came to Him and said, "Lord, how often shall my brother sin against me, and I forgive him? Up to seven times?" 22 Jesus said to him, "I do not say to you, up to seven times, but up to seventy times seven.*

DIVORCE

You feel:

- Unlovable
- Helpless
- Sorrowful
- That you failed your kids and family

Solution:

Marriage between a man and a woman is an eternal covenant ordained by God that, if broken, has far-reaching implications into the lives of the ones affected.

> *Marriage is a sanctified relationship that for all intents and purposes is eternal.*

The death of a partner is the only way a marriage should end. Although, there is precedent that if abuse is going on then the marriage may need to end. Divorce is the death of a relationship, and it is hard for all involved. God still loves you. If you desire to be married again, I believe God can send you another spouse.

> *1 Corinthians 7:2 KJV - Nevertheless, to avoid fornication, let every man have his own wife, and let every woman have her own husband.*

TROUBLED CHILDREN

You feel:

- That you failed as a parent
- You let down God
- Helpless
- Legal issues and behavioral issues compound the feelings of guilt and shame

Solution:

Pray for them. You raised them the best you could do. Commit them to the Lord, and let Him awaken their hearts to His wisdom.

> *Psalm 127:3-5 NKJV - 3 Behold, children [are] a heritage from the LORD, The fruit of the womb [is] a reward. 4 Like arrows in the hand of a warrior, So [are] the children of one's youth. 5 Happy [is] the man who has his quiver full of them; They shall not be ashamed, But shall speak with their*

enemies in the gate.

BEING SINGLE

You feel:

- Nobody wants you
- There is no soul mate for you
- God has forgotten about you

Solution:

Be content in whatever state you are in. If you desire to be married, then ask God to make you an able partner for your future spouse. Have him prepare your heart to be married. Read books on marriage and seek counsel from leaders in your life.

1 Corinthians 7:27 KJV - Art thou bound unto a wife? seek not to be loosed. Art thou loosed from a wife? seek not a wife.

DEPRESSION OR MENTAL TROUBLE

You feel:

- God did not create a good life for you
- You do not have a strong will to live
- You do not know why God created you

Solution:

Trust that God is good. He wants the best for your life.

He created you for this specific season in time.

You are valuable to Him. He has need of you and your gifts.

> *Psalm 139:14-18 NKJV - 14 I will praise You, for I am fearfully [and] wonderfully made; Marvelous are Your works, And [that] my soul knows very well. 15 My frame was not hidden from You, When I was made in secret, [And] skillfully wrought in the lowest parts of the earth. 16 Your eyes saw my substance, being yet unformed. And in Your book they all were written, The days fashioned for me, When [as yet there were] none of them. 17 How precious also are Your thoughts to me, O God! How great is the sum of them! 18 [If] I should count them, they would be more in number than the sand; When I awake, I am still with You.*

WISDOM FROM THE BIBLE ON BEING ALONE

The Bible has great wisdom on being alone. Look at these promises from God that you can experience today. He is faithful to help you if you want Him to.

HE WILL NEVER LEAVE YOU

Hebrews 13:5 ESV - Keep your life free from love of money, and be content with what you have, for he has said, "I will never leave you nor forsake you

CAST YOUR CARE. YOU ARE NOT ABLE TO BEAR THE BURDEN.

1 Peter 5:7 KJV - Casting all your care upon Him; for He careth for you.

KNOW YOU ARE FLYING. HE IS HOLDING YOU UP.

Psalms 34:18 KJV - The LORD is nigh unto them that are of a broken heart; and saveth such as be of a contrite spirit.

HE HOLDS YOU BY HIS RIGHT HAND. YOU ARE NOT ABANDONED. YOU ARE NOT LEFT OUT.

Psalms 73:23 KJV - Nevertheless I am continually with thee: thou hast holden me by my right hand.

GOD'S SHEEP DOGS (GOODNESS AND MERCY) ARE WITH YOU. YOU ARE NEVER ALONE. YOUR FAITHFUL GOD IS ALWAYS ON YOUR SIDE.

Psalm 23:4-6 NKJV - 4 Yea, though I walk through the valley of the shadow of death, I will fear no evil; For You [are] with me; Your rod and Your staff, they comfort me. 5 You prepare a table before me in the presence of my enemies; You anoint my head with oil; My cup runs over. 6 Surely goodness and mercy shall follow me All the days of my life; And I will dwell in the house of the LORD Forever.

There is no guarantee you will not feel like you are doing it all by yourself. You can only fly alone if you rely on the Holy Spirit. He gives you Grace to accomplish infinitely more than you could in your own strength.

SPREAD YOUR WINGS AND SOAR

1 Corinthians 15:10 KJV - But by the grace of God I am what I am: and His grace which was bestowed upon me was not in vain; but I labored more abundantly than they all: yet not I, but the grace of God which was with me.

SUMMARY

In summary, God has called you to be an eagle that soars alone. You are uniquely gifted. You have to be you and not somebody else. If you want to compare scars, I have gone through my fair share of trials. I have lost a child. I lost a brother when I was twelve. I lost my mother and my father. I know about pain, hurt, and loss. However, I also know that God is my Comforter. He is able to give me the strength I need to persevere: alone if I must, and He will do the same for you. I know that you are able to fly alone, for you are an eagle, and that is what they do. Fly solo, you mighty eagle.

PRAYER

Father, in the name of Jesus, I thank You for Your precious people. I thank You for Your soldiers. Thank You, God, for the eagles who are developing. I thank You for the Eagle's nest that You are allowing us to form. Thank You for raising up world-changers! Thank You for helping us to not be afraid or ashamed to do whatever You have called us to do.

Help us to understand the uniqueness You have placed in us. Help us right now to know our value, and to know that we mean something to You. Show us our place in the Body of Christ. Allow us to know that we are special in Your eyes. We rely on You God to support us as we soar alone in our divine destinies. We bless You and give You all the praise. In the name of Jesus Christ I pray. Amen.

CHAPTER 10

CONTRASTING COLORS

CANNOT IGNORE AN EAGLE

Due to their striking appearance, you can recognize an eagle from a far distance. Their curved beaks, their imposing size, their long talons, and their distinctive color palette all make for an easily identifiable creature. Eagles do not blend in to their environment; they were not made to, for they are apex predators. They exist at the top of the food chain. Full-grown eagles have no natural predators. We also, as God's eagles, are recognizable from a distance due to the anointing on our lives. We stand out. We do not blend in. We are seen from a far distance. We are apex predators able to take down the enemies of our Lord.

> ◊ We have no natural predators due to the ◊
> victory we live in through Christ.

HOLY SPIRIT ALL OVER YOU

Have you ever noticed a stranger from far away? Something about them piqued your interest. Maybe it was something about their appearance, something you heard them say, or perhaps you sensed something else about them. They stood out because of their attributes. In the same way, anointed believers that have a fierce dedication to the Lord have a light that shines about them. It is like the glow of a low-wattage light bulb. These people have tapped into the power and presence of the Holy Spirit. He shows up visibly on them. We can all wear the Holy Spirit in a way that makes us noticeable; just like the attributes of the eagle that make it stand out from other animals.

The Bald Eagle has two primary body colors; brown and white. I believe that the dark feathers of the Bald Eagle symbolically represent our outside physical being. The white head is like the light of the Holy Spirit being shone through the anointing of God. We can understand then, that we can let the anointing of God so alight in us that it becomes visible. He will be seen in us and on us.

> **People with close relationships to God, exude a brilliant light.**

You can sense or see them from far away. Jesus is lighting them up!

Matthew 5:14-16 ESV - 14 "You are the light of the world. A city set on a hill cannot be hidden. 15 Nor do people light a lamp and put it under a basket, but on a stand, and it gives light to all in the house. 16 In the same way, let your light shine before others, so that they may see your good works and give glory to your Father who is in heaven.

We are like cities set on a hill. We cannot be hidden when we glow so bright. We are the light of the world. We must be shining the light of Christ to share the message of the Gospel.

EAGLES IN SCRIPTURE

I want to share with you some biblical examples of people walking in the anointing of God. You can see here that God wants us to walk boldly in our calling. We will be noticeable from a far distance if we take these following encouragements to heart.

JOSEPH AND THE COAT OF MANY COLORS.

Genesis 37:3-11 ESV - 3 Now Israel loved Joseph more than any other of his sons, because he was the son of his old age. And he made him a robe of many colors. 4 But when his brothers saw that their father loved him more than all his brothers, they hated him and could not speak peacefully to him. 5 Now Joseph had a dream, and when he told it to his brothers they hated him even more. 6 He said to them, "Hear this dream that I have dreamed: 7 Behold, we were binding sheaves in the field, and behold, my sheaf arose and stood upright. And behold, your sheaves gathered around it and bowed down to my sheaf." 8 His brothers said to him, "Are you indeed to reign over us? Or are you indeed to rule over us?" So they hated him even more for his dreams and for his words. 9 Then he dreamed another dream and told it to his brothers and said, "Behold, I have dreamed another dream. Behold, the sun, the moon, and eleven stars were bowing down to me." 10 But when he told it to his father and to his brothers, his father rebuked him and said to him, "What is this dream that you have dreamed? Shall I and your mother and your brothers indeed come to bow ourselves to the ground before you?" 11 And his brothers were jealous of him, but his father kept the saying in mind.

Joseph was so dearly loved by his father. He was the son of Rachel, the wife that he loved more than his others. He would see Joseph and be reminded of her bringing him joy to know she lives on. He was the favorite son: the golden child. We are all favorites of our Father. He has made us a robe of righteousness that makes us stand out in the world.

However, Joseph brought trouble on himself. He shared the dreams that the Lord gave him, but it was not the right time. There are things that should not be shared with others. Not everyone can receive what God has told you.

⬦   **Protect your anointing.**   ⬦

Do not be reckless with what God has given you. Be humble and submit to the leading of the Holy Spirit. He will let you know if and when to share.

Joseph, in his innocence, knew he was the favorite child of his father. He grew up with this favoritism. He might not have ever faced hardship; he was only 17-years old. He might have thought himself invincible; a prototypical spoiled child. Surely his father would protect him if something went awry. Proverbs 16:18, paraphrased, says that pride comes before a fall. Pride will lead us to say and do dumb things. We must always be humble and stay submitted to God. Even the world detests a prideful spirit!

The favoritism his father showed him drove a wedge between Joseph and his brothers; they hated him. They desired to be loved too. You must know that the world will hate us for being loved of God. They will see your blessings and be jealous of you. They will see God work things out in your life and think it is not fair. They will try to do things their way and get nowhere, and then blame you for doing the same thing under the guidance of the Holy Spirit and it flourishes.

The world as a whole will reject you and will try to push you down. They do not want Jesus, but they want His blessings. People will try to use you for your anointing. They will try to get close to you and manipulate you because you have something they cannot get. When that does not work, they will try to harm you with their words and actions. You need to be harmless as a dove (gentle) but wise as a serpent (know when to retreat).

> Our anointing is too important for us to allow the enemy to distract us as we do God's work.

We as eagles must be willing to stand out in righteousness and fly away from even the appearance of evil.

Joseph had a strong calling on his life. He was the favorite son. He knew he was the favorite son. You are God's favorite eagle, and as such you have an anointing that no one else does. There is no comparison between you and someone else. You are unique and distinct. You cannot allow yourself to get a big head full of prideful thinking. God cannot work through a prideful child! Joseph went through trials because of his demeanor. All the things he went through taught him to be humble. God could then use him to save Israel and Egypt.

Joseph never forgot who he was. His father taught him about the faithfulness of God. Do not forget that you belong to God. He paid a high price to have you. He values you and wants you to value yourself and Him. There are timings to God's plans in our lives, and we must not get impatient: thinking we have to make something happen. Follow God and He will show you when and what to do. No matter if the entire world is against you; you can be confident in what God has given you.

Be humble, you eagle, submit yourself to God, and watch as the anointing in your life opens doors that no man can shut. Who but God could take a man from prison and make him the second-in-command of a country?! Promotion follows those who follow the Lord. In due time, you will reap a harvest for your good work in the Lord. Until then, remain humble, for humility shines the light of God. Others will see God in you from miles away because of that light of humility.

ELI AND SAMUEL.

1 Samuel 3:1-11 CEV - 1-2 Samuel served the Lord by helping Eli the priest, who was by that time almost blind. In those days, the Lord hardly ever spoke directly to people, and he did not appear to them in dreams very often. But one night, Eli was asleep in his room, 3 and Samuel was sleeping on a mat near the sacred chest in the Lord's house. They had not been asleep very long 4 when the Lord called out Samuel's name. "Here I am!" Samuel answered. 5 Then he ran to Eli and said, "Here I am. What do you want?" "I didn't call you," Eli answered. "Go back to bed." Samuel went back. 6 Again the Lord called out Samuel's name. Samuel got up and went to Eli. "Here I am," he said. "What do you want?" Eli told him, "Son, I didn't call you. Go back to sleep." 7 The Lord had not spoken to Samuel before, and Samuel did not recognize the voice. 8 When the Lord called out his name for the third time, Samuel went to Eli again and said, "Here I am. What do you want?" Eli finally realized that it was the Lord who was speaking to Samuel. 9 So he said, "Go back and lie down! If someone speaks to you again, answer, 'I'm listening, Lord. What do you want me to do?' " Once again Samuel went back and lay down. 10

SPREAD YOUR WINGS AND SOAR

Contrasting Colors | Chapter 10

The Lord then stood beside Samuel and called out as he had done before, "Samuel! Samuel!" "I'm listening," Samuel answered. "What do you want me to do?" 11 The Lord said: Samuel, I am going to do something in Israel that will shock everyone who hears about it!

Eli was of the lineage of Aaron, the High Priest of the Israelites. He was taught about all the wonderful things God did for His people while they were in the wilderness. He attempted to live as holy as he could. He was in charge of the tabernacle; but he had two wicked sons that did not respect God. There was a prophecy given to Eli that said his sons would surely die and that his family shall be cut off.

⧫ **God takes holy business seriously!** ⧫

Samuel, one of the greatest priests/prophets of the Old Testament, was under his care. Samuel's mother, Hannah, dedicated him to the Lord's house in Shiloh. Shiloh was the location of the Tabernacle. Hannah promised to give to God the first child she birthed. When she became pregnant and weaned Samuel, she brought him to Eli to be of service to the Lord. He became his assistant.

**We must always remember
that God is faithful.**

He saw that Hannah was afflicted in her heart. When she humbly prayed to God and Eli gave her his blessing, she was able to conceive.

God hears our prayers. We do not serve an uncaring and unloving God that is disinterested in us. No! He is intimately intune with our every need and is so desiring to provide for us as a good father would. We have the prayers of intercession and agreement of Jesus giving us His blessing. 2 Corinthians 1:20 tells us that all the promises of God in Christ Jesus are, yes, and in Him, amen. We agree with His Word, and we receive as we believe.

When God began speaking to the young child, Eli discerned that it was the Lord that was talking. Believers that are more advanced in their walk with the Lord need to be guiding the less experienced. We need anointed teachers that can lead us in the right way. Eli taught everything Samuel needed to know - until the Lord was able to teach him directly.

1 Samuel 3:19-21 CEV - 19 As Samuel grew up, the Lord helped him and made everything Samuel said come true. 20 From the town of Dan in the north to the town of Beersheba in the south, everyone in the country knew that Samuel was truly the Lord's prophet. 21 The Lord often appeared to Samuel at Shiloh and told him what to say.

SPREAD YOUR WINGS AND SOAR

God established His Word through Samuel. Everyone knew he was the Lord's prophet. Why is that? It could be that Eli was telling everyone about Samuel. He knew that Samuel was hearing from God. Eli could have encouraged Samuel to speak out to others. Even today, the older believers should be supporting the younger believers to step out and do what God has called them to do.

Prophets were a rare commodity at that time. When a true one was identified - people took notice. The relationship that Samuel built with the Lord led to the Lord glorifying him.

> **Your relationship with God will take you places no one else can.**

He will lead you where you need to go. You will look back on your life (maybe even right now) and see how remarkable it is to be where you are! We can take no credit. It is all because of Christ's infinite grace and boundless mercy that we are able to know the Father.

> **The more you invest into your relationship with God, the greater the return will be.**

You will make more forward progress in your life as you seek God above all else. As an eagle, when you fly closer to God, the resulting glow that you receive from the anointing shall be seen from far away. People will take notice just like they did with Samuel.

ELISHA AND ELIJAH.

2 Kings 8:8-14 CEV - 8 When they got there, Elijah took off his coat, then he rolled it up and struck the water with it. At once a path opened up through the river, and the two of them walked across on dry ground. 9 After they had reached the other side, Elijah said, "Elisha, the Lord will soon take me away. What can I do for you before that happens?" Elisha answered, "Please give me twice as much of your power as you give the other prophets, so I can be the one who takes your place as their leader." 10 "It won't be easy," Elijah answered. "It can happen only if you see me as I am being taken away." 11 Elijah and Elisha were walking along and talking, when suddenly there appeared between them a flaming chariot pulled by fiery horses. At once, a strong wind took Elijah up into heaven. 12 Elisha saw this and shouted, "Israel's cavalry and chariots have taken my master away!" After Elijah had gone, Elisha tore his clothes in sorrow. 13 Elijah's coat had fallen off, so Elisha picked it up and walked back to the Jordan River. 14 He struck the water with the coat and wondered, "Will the Lord perform miracles for me as he did for Elijah?" As soon as Elisha did this, a dry path opened up

{ *through the water, and he walked across.* }

Elijah was the mentor to Elisha. God called Elisha out specifically. Elijah went down to where Elisha was and cast his mantle over him to signify that he was now under his tutelage. Elisha quickly dropped everything (he was farming), said goodbye to his parents, used the wood from his plow to boil the oxen he was using, celebrated with his village, and then left to minister unto Elijah.

For about six years, Elisha walked with, talked with, and worked with Elijah as his assistant. He saw mighty miracles done in the name of the Lord. He was taught directly by one of the most powerful prophets of the Old Testament. He saw the light that Elijah brought. Elijah's anointing could be seen from a distance.

Elisha, however, wanted the double-portion. He chose to stick to his mentor's side. He was there and watched his spiritual father ascend in a whirlwind of wondrous splendor! Elisha was touched by his emotions for a bit, but then he dusted himself off and picked up the mantle left behind. He was determined to walk in the things of God. We also, as Christ's disciples are able to pick up the mantle of our Mentor, Jesus Christ, and walk in the things He has shown us. We must - if we expect to make any sort of impact for Jesus. Take up His mantle (cross) daily and follow

Him.

◇◇ **People will see Jesus all over you.** ◇◇

You will be noticeable from a distance, for Jesus will draw all those around you to Himself.

PAUL AND TIMOTHY.

2 Timothy 2:1-7 CEV - 1 Timothy, my child, you must let Christ Jesus make you strong by His gift of undeserved grace. 2 You have often heard me teach. Now I want you to tell these same things to followers who can be trusted to tell others. 3 As a good soldier of Christ Jesus you must endure your share of suffering. 4 Soldiers on duty don't work at outside jobs. They try only to please their commanding officer. 5 No one wins an athletic contest without obeying the rules. 6 And farmers who work hard are the first to eat what grows in their field. 7 If you keep in mind what I have told you, the Lord will help you understand completely.

Paul is known as one of the greatest apostles in history. He wrote two-thirds of the New Testament! He traveled 1,000's of miles to preach the Gospel of Jesus Christ. He established over 10 churches (some sources indicate possibly 20) throughout his lifetime. He walked in the power of the Holy Spirit. His teachings even today are so rich and full of the Spirit of God.

Paul, being a traveling missionary and apostle, saw a lot of people. Some of these men he took under his own wing, seeing the same zeal that he had for the Lord. One of those men is Timothy. Timothy had traveled with Paul and got hands-on schooling from him. He shared in the same victories and also imprisonments. He and Paul were close. In the book of 2 Timothy, Timothy was the Bishop of the largest church in the world at that time: Ephesus. There were a whole lot of people to shepherd, and especially as a young man, this was a major undertaking. He needed the encouragement he could only get from his mentor. What does Paul tell him?

- Let Christ strengthen you. Rely on His grace.
- Teach those things you have heard to others who are able to teach.
- You must be ready to endure suffering, for all believers will be persecuted and tried.
- Do not please men, but instead look to please Your Commanding Officer, Jesus Christ, like a good soldier.
- Obey the commandments of the Christian life just like an athlete that obeys the rules in their sport. Then, you will give yourself the opportunity to experience victory.
- Know that the fruits of your labor will come

to you first. You shall receive a harvest of what you have planted, just like a farmer who tends his soil and plants his seed.

- Do not forget these words; God will help you understand what they truly mean.

If we follow these guidelines, we will be amplifying the anointing of God on our lives. You will be noticeable from far away. Let your true colors be seen, eagle.

EVENT THAT SHAPED THE WORLD 🦅
Azusa Street Revival, LA

Services conducted by Pastor William J. Seymour in a small holiness mission on Azusa St. birthed a global spiritual renewal. When the revival started, 1000's converged on the city from all over the world to attend. They found a renewed sense of purpose by being saved, sanctified, and filled with the Holy Spirit with the evidence of speaking in other tongues. All color lines were washed away. In one meeting, over 20 nationalities were counted. Fine ladies could be found lying on the floor next to domestic servants and washerwomen. Prominent churchmen and government officials sat next to field hands. It was the great social equalizer for race, gender, age, and class.

"Revival is like a fire that is carried by the wind - its sparks will ignite the dry wood in every direction it blows." - William J. Seymour

"The impact from this small seed is continuing. Through this Pentecostal Revival and subsequent Charismatic Renewal, more ministers, missionaries, churches have been planted, and people brought to salvation than any other movement in church history. Soon the numbers of those impacted will eclipse all other religious movements put together." - Rick Joyner

EAGLES OF THE FAITH

I want to spotlight some true anointed eagles from our history. History can attest to the fruit of the labor that God has worked out through these powerful men and women. We can honor what God has done and thank Him for the contributions these brothers and sisters have made for the sake of the Gospel

BISHOP G'T. HAYWOOD

Haywood, who was African-American,

was born to Bennett and Pennyann Haywood in Greencastle, Indiana, in 1880 and moved to Haughville, a neighborhood in Indianapolis, at the age of three. As a child, he attended School 52 and then Shortridge High School. Haywood was employed by the Indianapolis Freeman and Indianapolis Recorder newspapers as a cartoonist.

In 1909, Haywood founded Christ Temple Church. Haywood's influence crossed ethnic boundaries, and by 1913, Christ Temple had a bi-racial congregation of 400 to 500, which later grew to 1500.

Around 1915, Haywood received a copy of Frank Ewart's paper Meat in Due Season, which argued for Jesus' Name doctrine. In response, Haywood invited the evangelist Glenn A. Cook to preach at Christ Temple, resulting in Haywood being re-baptized "In the Name of Jesus" and he in turn re-baptized 465 members of his congregation. Thus facilitating the spread of Oneness Pentecostalism throughout Indiana.

The third general council of the Assemblies of God convened in October 1915, and primary on the agenda was a debate on the merits of the new Jesus'-name doctrine vs the traditional trinitarian doctrine. Haywood and E. N. Bell spoke on behalf of the Jesus' Name doctrine, and Collins and Jacob Miller spoke against. The result was a draw, and it was agreed to readdress the topic at the fourth general council in October 1916. At the fourth general council a statement of faith was enacted which soundly rejected Jesus'-name doctrine causing just over one fourth of the ministers to leave the Assemblies of God. In 1911, Haywood had become affiliated with the Pentecostal Assemblies of the World (PAW) and after his conversion helped convert the organization to Oneness Pentecostalism.

Many of the former Assemblies of God ministers that left in 1916 formed the General Assembly of the Apostolic Assemblies, which at the start of World War I merged with the PAW in order for its ministers to obtain noncombatant statues. The new and interracial organization appointed Haywood as its general chairman. By 1924, the PAW split on racial lines due to logistical and social problems created by Jim Crow laws, and Haywood was appointed Bishop of the newly reorganized PAW.

Haywood composed many gospel songs including "Jesus, the Son of God", "I See a Crimson Stream of Blood", and "Do All in Jesus' Name". Many of his songs were published in The Bridegroom Songs, which was published by Christ Temple. Haywood was also an author and Oneness apologist. He wrote tracts, such as "The Victim of the Flaming Sword" and "The Finest of Wheat" as well as published "The Voice in the Wilderness", a publication that became the official organ of the Pentecostal Assemblies of the World in 1925.

Upon his death in 1931, Haywood was interred in Crown Hill Cemetery. In 1980, the city of Indianapolis designated the segment of Fall Creek Drive where Christ Temple is located as "Bishop Garfield T. Haywood Memorial Way" in his honor.

BISHOP R.C. LAWSON

Robert Clarence Lawson was born on May 5, 1883 in New Iberia, Louisiana. His parents died when he was very young and he was raised by an aunt, Peggy Fraser, during his early childhood.

Lawson had no plans to enter the ministry; he did have plans to become a lawyer and businessman. After attending Howe Institute (New Iberia) in Louisiana, Lawson traveled throughout the United States, becoming a cabaret singer and gambling and hustling when he had the chance.

In 1913, Lawson was stricken ill while in the Midwest and was diagnosed with tuberculosis. At that time, this diagnosis was tantamount to a death sentence, and doctors felt that nothing could be done to save his life.

While in the hospital, Lawson was ministered to by an elderly woman whose son was hospitalized in the same room. A "Holy Ghost Woman", as he described her, who urged him to start praying. She belonged to the Apostolic Faith Assembly pastored by Elder G.T. Haywood.

In later life, Lawson enjoyed telling the story of his call of God to the ministry: "As I was kneeling beside the bed saying my prayers, suddenly there entered the room the presence of God in a whirlwind. This presence enveloped me while I lay upon my bed, and the voice of God spoke out of a whirlwind in words I distinctly heard, saying, 'Go preach My Word. I mean you…I mean you…I mean YOU. Go preach My Word.'"

A short time later, the frail young man was healed and followed his divine orders by heading the Apostolic Faith Assembly in Indianapolis and becoming baptized. When Lawson first became, "saved," he belonged to a Pentecostal church.

That year, Lawson founded the Refuge Church of Christ in 1919, after members of a prayer band in Harlem welcomed him and turned their meetings over to him. That small church grew and became known as Refuge Temple, and, later, the Greater Refuge Temple. At its height, the enterprise on 133rd Street contained a grocery store, a bookstore, record and radio shop, and daycare. In the basement of the church was a complete printing office, where many tracts, booklets, and songs were published.

The Greater Refuge Temple in Harlem, New

York City has been located since 1945 in a former casino and vaudeville/movie theater. The building was renovated and had its colorful facade added in 1966.

The Refuge Temple in Harlem was the hub of Lawson's evangelistic efforts in the Northeast, which ultimately grew into the Church of Our Lord Jesus Christ, or COOLJC. Lawson's field work took him up and down the East Coast, throughout the West Indies, and as far as West Africa, where Lawson appointed missionaries to carry on the church's spiritual work.

Lawson was a leading figure in an influential Pentecostal organization at a time when Pentecostal churches were rare. Lawson founded a chain of funeral homes, a seminary, a radio station, a magazine, and several businesses, among other endeavors.

By the time Lawson died on June 30, 1961, membership at his headquarters, Greater Refuge Temple, had grown to over 3,000 members. Lawson's Harlem church is still thriving more than 45 years after his death.

In 1998, COOLJC had about 30,000 members in 450 churches in the United States. There are now 582 churches worldwide, including congregations in West Africa, Mexico, Canada, the British West Indies, the Dominican Republic, England, Haiti, and the Philippines. Its U.S. membership remains predominantly African-American.

LESTER SUMRALL

Lester Sumrall was a man who threw himself at the feet of Jesus Christ, possessing a zeal and commitment to God that still amazes those who knew him.

Lester Sumrall (1913-1996) was a world-renowned pastor and evangelist, entering full-time service for God after experiencing a dramatic and life-altering encounter with Jesus Christ. At the age of 17, as he lay on a deathbed suffering from tuberculosis, he received a vision. Suspended in midair to the right of his bed was a casket; on his left was a large open Bible. He heard these words: "Lester Sumrall, which of these will you choose tonight?" He made his decision – he would preach the Gospel as long as he lived. When Lester Sumrall awoke the next morning, he was completely healed and served the Lord for sixty-five years. Lester Sumrall traveled the world ministering in 110 countries, including Soviet Siberia, Russia, Tibet, and China. During his life he penned over 130 books.

In 1957 Lester Sumrall, with the help and support of his family and friends, founded LeSEA (Lester Sumrall Evangelistic Association), a ministry which has subsequently given birth to well over 100 books and study guides, eleven television stations, a satellite ministry, three FM radio stations, five shortwave stations reaching over ninety percent of the world's population, and a quarterly magazine. In 2018, LeSEA Broadcasting changed its name to Family Broadcasting Corporation (FBC).

In 1987, at the age of 74, Dr Sumrall founded LeSEA Global Feed The Hungry, aimed at wiping out hunger among those struggling to survive amidst poverty, famine, disaster, and war.

OTHER EAGLES OF THE GOSPEL

- Smith Wigglesworth (1859–1947) Pentecostalism
- William J. Seymour (1870–1922) Azusa Street Revival
- Charles Parham (1873–1929) Speaking in tongues
- F. F. Bosworth (1877–1958)
- Aimee Semple McPherson (1890–1944) Foursquare Church
- William Branham (1909–1965) Faith Healer, prophet
- Kathryn Kuhlman (1907–1976) Faith Healer
- A. A. Allen (1911–1970)

- Derek Prince (1915–2003) Faith, spiritual warfare, demonology
- Kenneth E. Hagin (1917–2003) Word of Faith
- Jack Coe (1918–1956)
- Oral Roberts (1918–2009) Oral Roberts University
- William L. Bonner (1921-2015) Apostle of Church of Our Lord Jesus Christ
- Yiye Ávila (1925–2013)
- Morris Cerullo (1931–2020) Pentecostalism, evangelist
- Jimmy Swaggart (1935–) Assemblies of God
- David Yonggi Cho (1936–) Yoido Full Gospel Church, Assemblies of God Discipleship, church Growth
- Jim (1940–) Tammy Baker (1942–2007) Assemblies of God televangelists
- Reinhard Bonnke (1940–2019) evangelist
- Ezekiel H. Guti (1960–) Forward in Faith Ministries International

SUMMARY

In summary, eagles are meant to stand out. They do not blend in with their surroundings. They have distinctive features that allow them to be easily identified from a distance. We as God's eagles have an anointing from the Holy Spirit that can be seen from a distance. We are the light of the world now. We cannot be hidden in darkness any longer!

> *Matthew 5:14-16 CEV - 14 You are the light for the whole world. A city built on top of a hill cannot be hidden, 15 and no one lights a lamp and puts it under a clay pot. Instead, it is placed on a lampstand, where it can give light to everyone in the house. 16 Make your light shine, so others will see the good you do and will praise your Father in heaven.*

We choose to submit ourselves to God and reject all pride like we learned from Joseph. We learn from those above us and trust in God's faithfulness like we learned from Samuel. We determine in ourselves to take up the mantle [cross] of Jesus and walk in His ways like we learned from Elisha. We can be good soldiers for Christ, enduring hardship, and not forsaking the teaching we have been taught as we learned from Timothy.

> *1 Peter 2:9-10 MSG - 9-10 But you are the ones chosen by God, chosen for the high calling of priestly work, chosen to be a holy people, God's instruments to do His work and speak out for Him, to tell others of the night-and-day difference He made for you—from nothing to something, from rejected to accepted.*

We learned from the lives of other eagles in the faith that you never know what kind of impact you will make when you choose God. You are God's holy, set apart, and anointed eagle. He has made you something from nothing. Before Christ, we were nobodies; we had no value, and we had no purpose. But God, in His love for us, took us into His own house. He gave His only Son that we might be able to know His heart. He defined our value. He showed us our purpose. We no longer exist in darkness. For the marvelous light of the Kingdom of God dwells on the inside of us! You must know that when you shine His light that others will take notice of you. Fly so you can be seen, you beautiful and radiant eagle.

PRAYER

Oh Father, in the name of Jesus, we come before You. We thank You. We praise You for making us stand out in this world. We give You the honor and the glory. For it is not by our own efforts that we can live holy. No, it is by Your Spirit that gives us the ability. You have anointed us to make an impact. We can no longer blend in like we used to. We can no longer sit under the table or hide ourselves away in caves. We are the light of the world and we shine because of the anointing that is placed on our lives.

We choose to draw closer to You. We choose

to submit ourselves to You. We choose to allow You to use us, however You need to. We choose to be seen today. In Jesus' holy name I pray. Amen.

CHAPTER 11

EXTREMELY BOLD

....

FEARLESS

Eagles are the most powerful and feared birds in the sky. They are bold and courageous. They will confront other birds and chase them away from carrion. When they exert their ferocity: most animals will flee. They are known to attack, rip the heads off, and eat the most venomous of snakes on land and in water. They are fearless fliers! In strong storms they fly in the opposite direction of the wind at their full strength. When most other birds would seek shelter or retreat - eagles take the storm head-on! Eagles have no fear.

What about you? Are you finding yourself facing a storm? Do you need to attack the venomous snakes slithering their way through your mind, heart, and spirit? I ask again, what about you?

EQUIPPED FOR BATTLE 

Eagles are more than equipped for their battles. Look at the sampling below to see some of these statistics. Do not mess with an eagle!

- Eagles have sharp beaks that can tear apart any kind of flesh
- They have talons that are about 3-4 inches long and sharp enough to cut deep into the flesh of their prey
- Grip strength of their talons
  - For comparison, an average human grip strength is 75 pounds
  - African Crowned Eagle: No official record but can crush skulls and spines of small mammals
  - Bald eagle: average 350 pounds
  - Golden Eagle: average 600 pounds
  - Harpy Eagle: average 550 pounds
  - Martial Eagle: No official record but able to break a human arm
- Eagles can carry 4-times their weight and take on prey many more times their own weight

Just like the eagle, we also are equipped for battle. Every soldier in God's army has a set of armor. God has not left us weaponless or defenseless!

**We have the armor of God
to stand firm in Him.**

Let us break down each piece of armor and how they help us be bold.

BE STRONG IN THE LORD

Ephesians 6:10 AMP - In conclusion, be strong in the Lord [draw your strength from Him and be empowered through your union with Him] and in the power of His [boundless] might.

We get our strength from our relationship with God. He is the empowering force in our lives.

The Holy Spirit enables us to walk in authority.

We have access to unlimited ability in Christ!

PUT ON YOUR ARMOR

Ephesians 6:11 AMP - Put on the full armor of God [for His precepts are like the splendid armor of a heavily-armed soldier], so that you may be able to [successfully] stand up against all the

> *schemes and the strategies and the deceits of the devil.*

The armor of God is for today. We need it to stand firm against Satan. We need it so we can be confident in God. We need it so we can be effective soldiers for Christ. What kind of soldier does not prepare themselves for battle? We are in a war with Satan, and we will be hurt without our armor. Put your armor on!

SPIRITUAL WARFARE

> *Ephesians 6:12 AMP - For our struggle is not against flesh and blood [contending only with physical opponents], but against the rulers, against the powers, against the world forces of this [present] darkness, against the spiritual forces of wickedness in the heavenly (supernatural) places.*

This war is not a physical one: it is spiritual. Right now, there is a war going on around us. We cannot see it, but we can see the effects of it. We are not fighting against humanity but against the spirits that control the way the world runs. Have you ever thought to yourself, "Why is the media corrupt?" "Why is the sanctity of marriage being questioned?" "Why are we not able to pray in schools?" The world is using every trick in the book to deceive our minds. These evil spirits are trying to get us to stand down and let them rule. If we do not stand up to them; we will never see positive change. Be ready to cast out devils. Put on your armor so you can make a difference in the world!

STAND YOUR GROUND

> *Ephesians 6:13 AMP - Therefore, put on the complete armor of God, so that you will be able to [successfully] resist and stand your ground in the evil day [of danger], and having done everything [that the crisis demands], to stand firm [in your place, fully prepared, immovable, victorious].*

Do you want to stand bold in the midst of the fight? Do you want to be used powerfully by God? Do you want to be a champion for the Lord? Do you want to hear Jesus tell you, "Well done, My good and faithful servant." It cannot happen unless you wear your armor.

TRUTH IS YOUR BELT

> *Ephesians 6:14a AMP - So stand firm and hold your ground, having tightened the wide band of truth (personal integrity, moral courage) around your waist...*

Truth is your belt. The truth of God's Word is what holds the armor together. With the truth in place, all the other pieces will fit together. The belt holds the scabbard for the sword and has pockets to carry various equipment. The truth gives you the tools to survive.

The belt must be tightened around the waist so that the armor moves as one piece. A loose-fitting belt does nobody any good! It would be more of a hindrance than anything else. The purpose of a belt is to prevent things from falling down. Do not allow the truth of God's Word to fall down in your life! You must hold fast to the truth of the Bible. Without truth you will be allowing all sorts of attacks from the enemy to hit you below the belt, where it can seriously injure you. Without truth, you will not be able to reproduce disciples for Christ. Gird your loins with truth! Do not be deceived by Satan's lies. You will not survive this battle if you do not trust God's Word as the truth that holds you together.

Knowing the truth will make you a bold soldier!

RIGHTEOUSNESS IS YOUR BREASTPLATE

Ephesians 6:14b AMP - ...and having put on the breastplate of righteousness (an upright heart),

SPREAD YOUR WINGS AND SOAR

The righteousness of God is your breastplate. It protects your heart and vital organs. We must know that we, through the blood of Jesus Christ, have been made righteous. Knowing you are righteous will make you bold in Him. You are holy; therefore, you can live holy because of Christ in you. The breastplate covers not just the front but wraps all around to the back as well. Knowing you are righteous will protect you from back attacks and sneak attacks! The enemy will not be able to assassinate your heart if you are protected by your righteous identity. Your character cannot be disproved. Your confidence in God is sure. No weapon raised against you will prosper. Believe that you are righteous today. Know that Christ paid the price of sin to purchase your heart. You can stand boldly because you know that Christ has made you righteous.

PEACE IS YOUR FOOTWEAR

Ephesians 6:15 AMP - and having strapped on your feet the gospel of peace in preparation [to face the enemy with firm-footed stability and the readiness produced by the good news].

The Gospel of peace is your footwear. The sandals the Roman army wore had nails hammered into the bottom of them. They would break these nails so only the studs remained. This gave them superior traction no matter the terrain. The abiding peace brought on by the Gospel will protect your feet. You will be able to move forward in victory. You will march forth over any kind of ground and be safe. You will be able to trek up steep hills and not falter. You will be able to progress in the war. You will not be left behind. You will be able to dig in your heels boldly and stand your ground to protect yourself and others from the evil of the day.

Another aspect we can look at is that we must always be ready to share the Gospel in the same way the Romans were always ready to move forward. We are to be ready at any time to give an answer for our faith. When we are unsure of what to say, then the Spirit will give us the words to boldly speak.

FAITH IS YOUR SHIELD

> *Ephesians 6:16 AMP - Above all, lift up the [protective] shield of faith with which you can extinguish all the flaming arrows of the evil one.*

Your faith in God is your shield. Faith is the substance of those things we hope for. Faith takes from the unseen and makes it visible. We call things that are not as though they are because in the spiritual realm they exist. Every shield is the same size because all have been given the measure of faith. The shield needed to be oiled each day so that it would not crack under heavy use or be affected by changes in weather. The oil they used would allow the shield to quench fiery arrows and also could make the enemy lose traction when their weapons struck it. The fiery darts of Satan are his lies and deceptions. You must keep your faith oiled by the anointing of the Holy Spirit to thwart these lies. Pray in the spirit, fellowship with God and believers, and diligently keep yourself in the Word of God to maintain your shield.

The shield could also be used in offense. The army would press forward and break enemy lines by battering them with their shields as one unit. The enemy line would fall apart, and the Romans would decimate them with their spears, swords, and daggers. Our faith in what God has said breaks through the enemy's lines! We are able to assault the things that come against us and route them through the faith we have. We cast down every vain imagination and evil thought that would attempt to take us down the wrong line of thinking. We have the faith to boldly conquer any obstacle because of Jesus!

SALVATION IS YOUR HELMET

Ephesians 6:17a AMP - And take the helmet of salvation,...

The helmet of salvation protects your mind. You have a future. You have a hope that is undying. You have an eternal home with Christ. What can succeed against our God? What can man do to us? When you have confidence that God is who He says He is, then your mind will be protected. Your vision, your hearing, your smelling, and tasting are safeguarded by the helmet of salvation. You can see God working. You can hear His voice. You can smell His goodness. You can taste His kindness. It all starts with your mind. What are you thinking about? Are you meditating on God's Word or on something else? What could be more important than God? Ask yourself that. The brain is the primary controller of the body. When you put on the helmet of Christ, He becomes Your Lord. You are submitted to His authority. He has the final say! Your helmet is backed by God's Word. You are not in this fight alone! He will give you the instructions you need to boldly succeed.

THE SPIRIT IS YOUR SWORD

Ephesians 6:17b AMP - ...and the sword of the Spirit, which is the Word of God.

The sword of the Spirit is the weapon that takes down our enemies. A soldier must go through training to learn how to wield their sword. We must also go through training to wield the sword of the Living Word of God. We diligently study the Bible to show ourselves approved. The Holy Spirit is our Instructor. He will teach us to use our sword in the most efficient and practical manner.

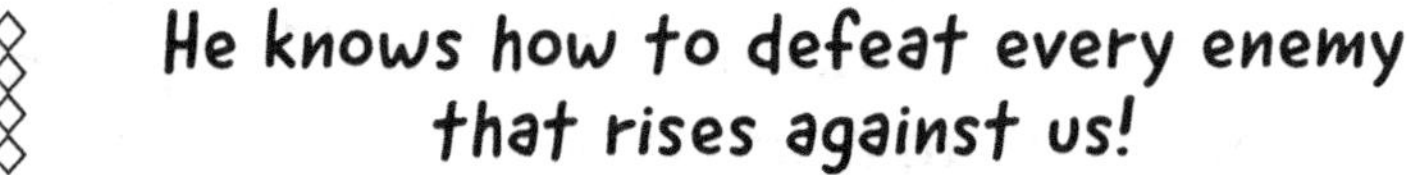

Sharpen your sword! Do not allow it to grow dull by ignoring your relationship with God! You have to keep your sword sharpened if you want to hurt your enemies. You will boldly cut through every adversary that rises against you when you put a priority on God's Word in your life.

PRAYER IS YOUR WILD CARD

Ephesians 6:18 AMP - With all prayer and petition pray [with specific requests] at all times [on every occasion and in every season] in the Spirit, and with this in view, stay alert with all perseverance and petition [interceding in prayer] for all God's people.

Prayer is like our wild card; it can do anything to affect the battlefield in our favor. Prayer can turn the tide. Prayer can send angels that will fight for you.

Prayer is a weapon that can strike the enemy from a distance. Prayer allows us to receive strategies and tactics from our General.

> **Prayer is what will make the difference between an ordinary soldier and a good soldier.**

Praying in the Spirit keeps our morale up. Praying and interceding on behalf of others will strengthen them. We need each others' prayers! We need unity in the ranks. Do not neglect prayer!

YOU ARE A FEARLESS EAGLE

With time, I have learned there is nothing to fear, because the One who now lives in me is greater than the one who lives in the world. Jesus has overcome the world; He has already won! Jesus lives in me; I can do all things because His loving wings of protection and victory are always on my side.

1 John 4:4 ESV - Little children, you are from God and have overcome them, for He who is in you is greater than he who is in the world.

SPREAD YOUR WINGS AND SOAR

Extremely Bold | Chapter 11

Courage requires boldness and strength; both of which come from God. He calls and commands us in His scriptures to be ready, to be bold in stepping out, and to make the choice to seek His aide. Ask, and it will be given unto you. We are called to be strong and courageous, to rise up and face whatever comes our way, for He is with us.

God is able to make you a strong and capable warrior who will conquer every obstacle that comes your way. God Himself, knows how to war and He knows how to teach us to do battle. This is why He has given us His armor: to fight and win. We are able to commit our loved ones to the Lord and He will watch over them. God does not lose any war. When we understand that God Almighty, the Lord of Angelic Armies, is for us, who can possibly be a threat to us?!

whom I take refuge, Who subdues my people under me.

What are you afraid of? Again, I ask, what about you? What storms are you currently facing? What lies are you allowing yourself to be corrupted by? Will you boldly step out, take courage, be strong in the Lord, and declare His victory!? For He is truly with you. Will you allow the God of all creation to transform you? Will you allow God to change your life from a timid and small bird who is cowering for shelter, and feels powerless and paralyzed by fear? Will you allow God to transform you into the regal, bold, courageous, and powerful creature you were born to be!? A fearless flier for Christ!? I pray that you do. For we need more fearless fliers in the army of God who will boldly take on any enemy.

SUMMARY

In summary, eagles are ferociously bold and powerful. Eagles prey on the most venomous of snakes. They fly into storm clouds head-on, unlike other birds that hide away. They have all the tools needed to be effective hunters and predators. We also have been given all the equipment we need to succeed in life. God is commanding all His soldiers to put on His armor. We must be ready to engage with demons, and to cast them out of people when necessary. Just like the eagle has no fear of any man, beast, or snake – in the same way we should have no fear of any demonic spirit, since we have God Himself on our side.

> **Greater is God inside of us than any other outside force.**

You are equipped to win in Christ. Put on your armor. Cast off all fear. Fly boldly, you powerful eagle.

PRAYER 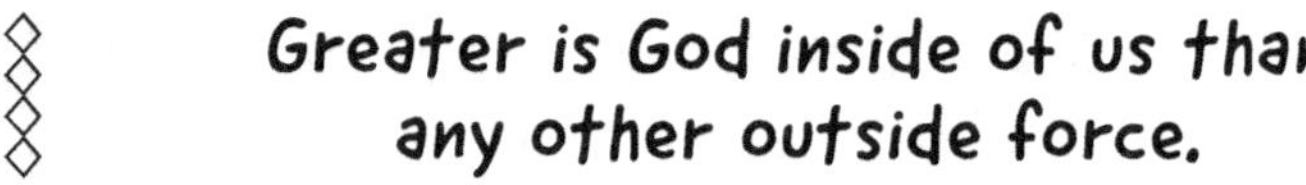

Father God in the name of Jesus, help us to see that You are with us. Strengthen, encourage, and embolden us. We want to fly over the storms that come our way. We want to take out every snake that dares to touch God's anointed. We want to be the fearless fliers You have called us to be! Remind us to seek You first and to choose to learn from You. So, that we can stand on Your holy Word with confidence and boldness. We are not afraid of anything that Satan or man can throw at us; for greater are You than he that is in the world. We thank You for never leaving our side and for giving us all the tools and equipment we need, to be bold. In Jesus' powerful name we pray. Amen.

CHAPTER 12

MASTERFUL FISHERMEN

....

GET READY TO FISH

Eagles must know how to catch fish to survive. Between 70% - 90% of a bald eagle's diet is made of fish. It is a good thing that God has given them all the tools to be masterful fishermen. They are able to see from far away, then strike at the perfect time. In the same way, we have been given all the tools we need to be masterful fishers of men.

Matthew 4:18-22 MSG - 18-20 Walking along the beach of Lake Galilee, Jesus saw two brothers: Simon (later called Peter) and Andrew. They were fishing, throwing their nets into the lake. It was their regular work. Jesus said to them, "Come with me. I'll make a new kind of *fisherman out of you. I'll show you how to catch men and women instead of perch and bass." They didn't ask questions, but simply dropped their nets and followed. 21-22 A short distance down the beach they came upon another pair of brothers, James and John, Zebedee's sons. These two were sitting in a boat with their father, Zebedee, mending their fishnets. Jesus made the same offer to them, and they were just as quick to follow, abandoning boat and father*

TWO TYPES OF FISHERMEN

There are two types of fishermen: commercial and recreational. We must understand that witnessing is our full-time job; it is not a hobby. The Word of God is our bait and net. We need God's help to sharpen our talents, abilities, and skills, to use the gifts He has given to us to catch the fish in our area.

Romans 11:29 AMP - For the gifts and the calling of God are irrevocable [for He does not withdraw what He has given, nor does He change His mind about those to whom He gives His grace or to whom He sends His call].

We are on assignment from God as His fishermen. We have been given an order to preach the Gospel to all. We must be vigilant so that we can rescue as many souls as possible. We would like all people to come to the saving knowledge of Jesus Christ.

> *Mark 16:15 AMP - And He said to them, "Go into all the world and preach the gospel to all creation.*

THE THREE-STEP PROCESS

I have broken down the fishing process into three steps. If we are committed, focused and prepared, then we can be successful fishers of men. Read on and take these truths to heart.

I: LOCK-IN / COMMITMENT

Before eagles lock-in on their targets, they have to decide which fish to go after. There are many factors which affect their choices, but ultimately they have to commit to one option. For us, this means having a strong commitment to God and whatever service He has called us into.

SPREAD YOUR WINGS AND SOAR

> *We must remain committed, steadfast, and immovable when it comes to what God has told us to do.*

We cannot be half-hearted if we expect to fulfill God's will in our lives. He is looking for those who will stay the course and glide on the Holy Spirit. We must choose to be committed to Him and His calling.

> *John 6:68-69 MSG - Peter replied, "Master, to whom would we go? You have the words of real life, eternal life. We've already committed ourselves, confident that you are the Holy One of God."*

Fishing can take awhile. You could be waiting hours for a bite. There is a level of dedication required to be a fisherman. If you jerk your fishing line too much, you will not get a bite. If you neglect to move your bait every so often, you will not get a bite. There is a level of understanding required if you want to be a great fisherman. When something is not working, what do you do? Do you give up? Do you stop because it is not working the way you want it to? Our God is faithful. When our fishing is not working we must be faithful to God's call.

> *Hebrews 10:23 AMP - Let us seize and hold tightly the confession of our hope without wavering, for He who promised is reliable and trustworthy and faithful [to His word];*

We ask Him for guidance and He will show us if we need to move to another spot, if we need to change our bait, if we need to get a different rod, or if we need to rest and let Him minister to us. Commit your ways to Him! God wants us to be successful fishermen just like eagles, and it starts with a commitment to follow Him.

> *Psalms 37:5 ESV - Commit your way to the Lord; trust in Him, and He will act.*

2: SWOOP DOWN / FOCUS

Next, the eagle swoops down to snatch their prey out of the water. It had its eye on the target from over a mile away! Eagles can strike blazingly fast and are quite accurate. In the same way, God wants our complete focus to be on Him and what He has told us. God is looking for follow-through. Let us look at the life of Daniel; for he represents this very thing.

Daniel was a prophet that focused on God's will above all else. He was blessed with unparalleled wisdom. He demonstrated the ability to interpret dreams and prophesy according to the spirit of the

Lord. The King recognized that he was special. The princes and other rulers were jealous of him, but they could find no fault in him.

Daniel 6:1-5 NKJV - 1 It pleased Darius to set over the kingdom one hundred and twenty satraps, to be over the whole kingdom; 2 and over these, three governors, of whom Daniel [was] one, that the satraps might give account to them, so that the king would suffer no loss. 3 Then this Daniel distinguished himself above the governors and satraps, because an excellent spirit [was] in him; and the king gave thought to setting him over the whole realm. 4 So the governors and satraps sought to find [some] charge against Daniel concerning the kingdom; but they could find no charge or fault, because he [was] faithful; nor was there any error or fault found in him. 5 Then these men said, "We shall not find any charge against this Daniel unless we find [it] against him concerning the law of his God."

They had decided the only way to trip him up was to persecute him for his faith. Daniel's faith in God was well-known. He had a routine and they could see that nothing made him deviate from it. They conspired together to make King Darius sign a proclamation that banned prayer to anyone except the King.

SPREAD YOUR WINGS AND SOAR

Daniel 6:6-9 NKJV - 6 So these governors and satraps thronged before the king, and said thus to him: "King Darius, live forever! 7 "All the governors of the kingdom, the administrators and satraps, the counselors and advisors, have consulted together to establish a royal statute and to make a firm decree, that whoever petitions any god or man for thirty days, except you, O king, shall be cast into the den of lions. 8 "Now, O king, establish the decree and sign the writing, so that it cannot be changed, according to the law of the Medes and Persians, which does not alter." 9 Therefore King Darius signed the written decree.

Daniel had no fear! He heard the proclamation and boldly opened his windows to show that he did not care what the circumstances were; he was going to pray. He cared more about what God thought than what anyone else did. He had a single focus to please the Lord.

Daniel 6:10 NKJV - Now when Daniel knew that the writing was signed, he went home. And in his upper room, with his windows open toward Jerusalem, he knelt down on his knees three times that day, and prayed and gave thanks before his God, as was his custom since early days.

SPREAD YOUR WINGS AND SOAR

The men were waiting for Daniel to pray. They watched him and knew they had caught him in the act of disobeying the King's royal decree. They thought they had won. The King was disheartened in himself. He did not know that Daniel prayed three times a day. He valued Daniel's wisdom and excellent spirit. He tried everything he could think of to rescue Daniel, but to no avail. Truly, these men were jealous because they were not able to provide the King with wisdom like Daniel. They did not realize they would be hurting the kingdom by removing one of the sources of wisdom and the voice of God from their midst. They were blinded by their hatred for Daniel, that they could not see they would be harming the kingdom too.

Our lives today are no different than Daniel's. When we decide to serve the Lord, Satan will set traps through others. He is going to try everything he can to derail you from your purpose.

> You must be focused on what God has asked you to do no matter who or what tries to get in your way.

Daniel 6:11-14 NKJV - 11 Then these men assembled and found Daniel praying and making supplication before his God. 12 And they went before the king, and spoke concerning the

> king's decree: "Have you not signed a decree that every man who petitions any god or man within thirty days, except you, O king, shall be cast into the den of lions?" The king answered and said, "The thing [is] true, according to the law of the Medes and Persians, which does not alter." 13 So they answered and said before the king, "That Daniel, who is one of the captives from Judah, does not show due regard for you, O king, or for the decree that you have signed, but makes his petition three times a day." 14 And the king, when he heard [these] words, was greatly displeased with himself, and set [his] heart on Daniel to deliver him; and he labored till the going down of the sun to deliver him.

The men made sure the King followed through. Written royal decrees were unchangeable. The King himself was even bound by the words. This King, though, had faith that Daniel's God could save him. He had seen that Daniel was not like the others. The things and feats that were done by Daniel could only be explained by God. The King could have thought, "Surely the same God that helped Daniel do all those things can save him from hungry lions on the verge of starvation?" This was the King's only hope.

Know that God gives us favor with our bosses, leaders, and teachers in spite of our enemies because of our faith in Him. We have favor with God and man when we keep His commandments. God is the

SPREAD YOUR WINGS AND SOAR

One in charge of promotion. He can make us look real good in front of our superiors! Keep your focus on the Lord and His calling, and He will bring forth promotion in your life.

Daniel 6:15-17 NKJV - 15 Then these men approached the king, and said to the king, "Know, O king, that [it is] the law of the Medes and Persians that no decree or statute which the king establishes may be changed." 16 So the king gave the command, and they brought Daniel and cast [him] into the den of lions. [But] the king spoke, saying to Daniel, "Your God, whom you serve continually, He will deliver you." 17 Then a stone was brought and laid on the mouth of the den, and the king sealed it with his own signet ring and with the signets of his lords, that the purpose concerning Daniel might not be changed.

The King was worried sick. He made a bold declaration that Daniel's God would save him, but he still had to get rid of his unbelief about it. He fasted and he could not sleep. It is possible he was praying too. He waited anxiously all night long until the sun came up. He had to know if Daniel was alive. To the King's joy, Daniel was alive! Daniel believed God would protect him because he trusted in Him. He had a single focus to do the will of God no matter what the circumstances were, and God made sure to preserve His life. God is the same today with us as He was with Daniel. When we allow Him to develop the characteristics of an eagle in us to be committed and focused, we will be protected by Him.

> *Daniel 6:18-23 NKJV - 18 Now the king went to his palace and spent the night fasting; and no musicians were brought before him. Also his sleep went from him. 19 Then the king arose very early in the morning and went in haste to the den of lions. 20 And when he came to the den, he cried out with a lamenting voice to Daniel. The king spoke, saying to Daniel, "Daniel, servant of the living God, has your God, whom you serve continually, been able to deliver you from the lions?" 21 Then Daniel said to the king, "O king, live forever! 22 "My God sent His angel and shut the lions' mouths, so that they have not hurt me, because I was found innocent before Him; and also, O king, I have done no wrong before you." 23 Now the king was exceedingly glad for him, and commanded that they should take Daniel up out of the den. So Daniel was taken up out of the den, and no injury whatever was found on him, because he believed in his God.*

To be a good fisher of men we must be focused on God and His calling. When we keep our focus on God, the rest will work itself out. Just like the eagle, swoop down and tackle the task God has given you with single-minded focus.

3: Clean your net / Preparation

Finally, we must clean our nets; we have to prepare ourselves to be used of God. We are going to take a step back now and see the preparation of the eagle. Early every morning, the eagle will preen its feathers for about an hour. Each feather will be checked for parasites, plucked if it has lost its ability to fly well, and coated with a liquid secreted from its mouth that makes the feathers water-resistant while also improving aerodynamics. It is preparing itself for the day ahead. In the same way, we must prepare our nets and rods, so that we can catch the people that God has placed in our path. We must be ready.

**We have the skills that we need
to win somebody to Christ.**

The lives of others are on the line! We have to know the Word to be able to teach the Word. We should be ready to give an answer for our faith.

2 Timothy 2:15 AMP - Study and do your best to present yourself to God approved, a workman [tested by trial] who has no reason to be ashamed, accurately handling and skillfully teaching the word of truth.

A fisherman has to watch their fishing pole. If the rod is set and they neglect to watch it, they may get a bite, but fail to reel it in. When we get bites, we need to pay attention so we can reel the catch in! The fisherman could lose their bait and not even know it. They have to check and maintain their equipment to make sure it is ready to catch fish. We want to be ready to catch opportunities the Lord sends our way.

> *2 Timothy 4:2 KJV - Preach the word; be instant in season, out of season; reprove, rebuke, exhort with all longsuffering and doctrine.*

Here are three ways we can prepare ourselves to be used by God.

Prayer

Prayer is an important part of our preparation for the day. Start your day with prayer to the Lord. Talk with God in the morning. Do not lose sight of how important communication with God is! Look below for practical examples of how we can approach God in the morning.

- Worship and praise Him because He is God all by Himself. He is sovereign and worthy of praise, glory, and honor for who He is.
- Thank Him for His goodness and kindness

towards you.

- Thank Him for the things He has done and is doing in your life.
- Declare your favorite verses.
- Read scripture and/or a devotional.
- Tell Him, "Good morning."
- Thank Him for waking you.
- Thank Him for the many blessings in your life. [Electricity, running water, shelter, nature, animals, clothing, family, friends, work, church]
- Turn on praise music.
- Sing your heart out to Him.
- Pray in the Spirit.

Let God arrange your day. Ask Him what He wants you to do today. He will let you know. Get your orders from the Lord in the morning to set your day up right. He knows what the day will bring. He will prepare you for its twists and turns. Do not neglect morning prayer time!

1 Thessalonians 5:16-18 AMP - 16 Rejoice always and delight in your faith; 17 be unceasing and persistent in prayer; 18 in every situation [no matter what the circumstances] be thankful and continually give thanks to God; for this is the

> *will of God for you in Christ Jesus.*
>
> *Psalms 118:24 KJV - This is the day which the Lord hath made; we will rejoice and be glad in it.*

Fasting

Fasting is another way in which we prepare ourselves. When we need to make important decisions, we may fast to receive and hear from the Lord clearly. Fasting makes the voice of God easier to discern in your heart. Fasting is not only from food or liquids, but also abstaining from anything that you consider a distraction. Fasting and praying is a powerful way to receive direction from God.

> *Acts 14:23 AMP - When they had appointed elders for them in every church, having prayed with fasting, they entrusted them to the Lord in whom they believed [and joyfully accepted as the Messiah].*

Seeking the Lord

Lastly, we must seek the Lord; choose to know who He is. Speak with and talk with Him like you would your friend. Take the time to study and show yourself approved. Read the Bible, read Christian books, listen to Christian radio, and watch Christian programming. This will grow your relationship with the Lord. Fellowship with like-minded believers and go to church. Believers should be receiving encouragement from each other. Remember your coworkers, friends, family, and the world's eyes are watching you. With God's help, you can live free from the influence of the world: a holy and righteous life. Let your light so shine before men, that they will glorify God in you, the same way the King did in Daniel's life. Seek the Lord in everything that you say and do. This will allow you to be sensitive to His leading, and help you to not miss the opportunities He sends your way.

Matthew 5:16 AMP - Let your light shine before men in such a way that they may see your good deeds and moral excellence, and [recognize and honor and] glorify your Father who is in heaven.

Colossians 3:17 AMP - Whatever you do [no matter what it is] in word or deed, do everything in the name of the Lord Jesus [and in dependence on Him], giving thanks to God the Father through Him.

WEIGHING THE FISH / MINISTERING

After catching a fish, the next step is to weigh it; you want to see what you are dealing with. This is the time for you to receive instruction from the Lord on how to best minister to the person now that you have caught them. Meditate on the Word, and let it sink deep into your heart, mind, and life. If you need guidance, do not be afraid to seek wise counsel from pastors and other leaders that have a strong foundation in God's Word.

Proverbs 3:5-6 AMP - 5 Trust in and rely confidently on the Lord with all your heart and do not rely on your own insight or understanding. 6 In all your ways know and acknowledge and recognize Him, and He will make your paths straight and smooth [removing obstacles that block your way].

We are able to give an answer for why we believe the way we do. Your personal testimony is one of the most powerful tools in your tackle box. You know what God has done in your life; be ready to share it. It might be exactly what another needed to hear.

SPREAD YOUR WINGS AND SOAR

> *1 Peter 3:15 AMP - But in your hearts set Christ apart [as holy—acknowledging Him, giving Him first place in your lives] as Lord. Always be ready to give a [logical] defense to anyone who asks you to account for the hope and confident assurance [elicited by faith] that is within you, yet [do it] with gentleness and respect.*

Do not be surprised if the person does not show growth immediately. It could take months or even years before you see the fruit of the Word you have given them. This is the part people hate: waiting. It takes time for people to grow, and for them to come from where they are to where they need to be. This process requires patience.

Seeds take time to grow. A farmer cannot plant a seed and expect a harvest the next day (without some sort of miracle). They have to diligently water the seed, nourish the seed, and protect the seed so that it can grow into a healthy plant. The seed takes patience to grow. Patience is simply the process of faith at work. The roots of a plant cannot be seen from the surface. For example, bamboo is a special plant. It can take up to three years for it to have a root system that is established enough for it to start growing rapidly on the surface, but once it becomes mature, the growth is evident. Do not lose heart! In due time, you shall see growth in the person.

If you do not see the growth you think should

be there, remember you are not the one doing the work: God is. He knows what He is doing, and He knows what needs to be done. He knows how long He wants to take to make whatever changes in the individual's life that need to happen. We do not know how deep the roots of despair, disappointment, pain, hurt, and even sin that is in the individual's life but God does. He knows how to go to the beginning of the source and bring about a healing restoration and deliverance.

Matthew 13:23 CEV - The seeds that fell on good ground are the people who hear and understand the message. They produce as much as 100 or 60 or 30 times what was planted.

I had this individual who kept giving me the runaround. I got fed up and told God, "I'm done with them!" But I realized, I cannot do that. We have no Heaven or Hell to put anyone into. We cannot give up on anyone because God did not give up on us. Compassion, patience, and love are requirements to be effective fishers of men.

1 Thessalonians 5:14 AMP - We [earnestly] urge you, believers, admonish those who are out of line [the undisciplined, the unruly, the disorderly], encourage the timid [who lack spiritual courage], help the [spiritually] weak, be very patient with everyone [always controlling your temper].

LEARN TO RELATE TO OTHERS

To catch different types of fish, you need different kinds of baits and nets. You have to learn how to relate to different types of people. Look at the life of Paul.

1 Corinthians 9:19-23 MSG - Even though I am free of the demands and expectations of everyone, I have voluntarily become a servant to any and all in order to reach a wide range of people: religious, nonreligious, meticulous moralists, loose-living immoralists, the defeated, the demoralized—whoever. I didn't take on their way of life. I kept my bearings in Christ—but I entered their world and tried to experience things from their point of view. I've become just about every sort of servant there is in my attempts to lead those I meet into a God-saved life. I did all this because of the Message. I didn't just want to talk about it; I wanted to be in on it!

Paul was a masterful fisherman. He became all things to all men. He knew how to relate to people. Do not just stay in your circle. Be willing to venture out. Paul was able to break down the Gospel enough to where he could use it to minister to anyone he came across. He understood the richness of the Gospel, and did not speak over their heads; but was able to speak and live it simply before all. He had the ability to connect to all kinds of individuals. We have not all been down the same roads, but we can find common ground. We have not all had the same experiences, but we can all share our struggles and victories with each other. We all have different testimonies, and God wants us to use those testimonies to encourage lives!

Jesus was able to talk to all types of people, sinners, the mentally-challenged, scribes, and religious leaders. He was able to relate to them because He knew what He had. He understood that reaching out was what the Father wanted Him to do. We also reach out because Jesus commands us to, and we desire to please Him.

> *John 5:19-20 MSG - So Jesus explained himself at length. "I'm telling you this straight. The Son can't independently do a thing, only what he sees the Father doing. What the Father does, the Son does. The Father loves the Son and includes him in everything he is doing.*

SPREAD YOUR WINGS AND SOAR

SUMMARY

In summary, we as masterful fishermen are able to take the Gospel to the lost. We have a commitment to the Lord to do His work. We should have a single-minded focus to follow through on what He has said. We have prepared ourselves to be used. We are able to reach out to those who have not yet surrendered to the Lord. We are able to witness and share the Word of the Lord. We can tell them that Jesus saves today.

Jesus is coming back for a people who have prepared themselves. We are called for such a time as this. Use the opportunities around you to share Jesus. Your friends and family should know that you are Christian. Now, I know, some people do not want to hear it, but what you can do… pray for them. Lift them up in prayer, cry out to God for them, ask the Lord to soften their hearts, help them to seek after Him, and most of all, live a God-fearing life before them. With the help of the Holy Spirit you are well-able to reel in a harvest for Jesus, you masterful eagle.

PRAYER

Father God, in the name of Jesus, we come before You. We desire to be masterful fishermen and masterful soul-winners. We desire to have the same mentality as the eagle. Help us right now to see men and women afar off that need to be witnessed to, that need to be spoken to through the power of the Holy Ghost. Give us the right words to say with the right attitude. Help us to direct them in the right path. Give us the insight of Your Word to be able to use it as a net, so that when we cast it out, souls will be saved and redeemed from darkness. Empower us to live a righteous and God-fearing life that pleases You and that draws men unto You. In the name of Jesus, we give You praise right now for doing it. In Jesus' precious name I pray. Amen.

CHAPTER 13

REVIEW

Well done! You made it to the end. I believe God has revealed many things to you about the eagle. Let us do a quick review of what we covered.

LIVE ON HIGH GROUND 

What does it mean for the Christian believer to live on high ground?

* * * * * * *

"Holiness, righteousness, salvation, and sanctification"

- We should want to live our lives holy, for He is holy

- Christ's great exchange of our sins with His complete righteousness
- We have been saved to live a life free from the bondage of sin
- We are being sanctified to live as people 'set apart'

SKILLED FLIERS

What are the three key things that allow the Christian to operate in God?

• • • • • • •

"Faith, belief, and the Holy Spirit"

- Our left wing is our faith in God
- Our right wing is our belief in God
- The wind thermal is the Holy Spirit that carries us

What is important about the believer being a skilled flier?

• • • • • • •

"Daily reliance on the Holy Spirit"

- Being led by the Holy Spirit
- Walk in the anointing
- Have confidence in God

EAGLES ARE MAJESTIC 

How does the majestic behavior of the eagle compare to us as Christian believers?

• • • • • • •

"Priests and kings in the Kingdom of God"

- All because of Jesus' sacrifice we are royalty due to our adoption into God's family
- We can minister to God wherever we are
- Approach His mercy seat boldly and often
- We are called to pray, make sacrifices, bless others and wear Christ

EAGLES HAVE TWO SETS OF VISION

What are the two sets of eyes that the Christian believer has?

• • • • • • •

"The believer has natural sight and spiritual sight"

- Desire to see with our spiritual eyes
- Walk in the spirit
- Look from proper perspective and vantage point of Christ's victory

VERY PATIENT

What is the definition of patience for a Christian believer?

• • • • • • •

"The ability to accept or tolerate delays, problems, or suffering without becoming anxious"

- God sees the 'big picture' knowing the beginning to the end
- Stay focused
- Valuable experiences through trials
- He is looking for us to believe, trust and depend on Him

NEST IN THE WILDERNESS

What does the wilderness mean for the Christian believer?

• • • • • • •

"The wilderness is the period of development and training"

- Preparation or a season for you to be trained, shaped, and molded into what God desires you to be
- Brought to a place for such a time as this
- Follow God's plans
- Allow these times (Seasons) to build you up, not tear you down
- Be encouraged that the wilderness is shaping you into what God desires you to be

EAGLES ARE FAITHFUL FOR LIFE

Why is faithfulness important to the Christian believer?

• • • • • • •

"Faithfulness builds character, endurance, and steadfastness"

- A few definitions of someone faithful is being loyal, constant, and demonstrating an allegiance that never falters
- God is looking for faithful followers
- God rewards those who are faithful in their callings and relationships

FLY ALONE

What should we learn from the fact that eagles fly alone?

• • • • • • •

"God has called us each individually and has a unique work for each of us to do"

- Many are called but few are chosen
- Follow God even when no one else does
- Recognize the seasons and seize the opportunities
- We are never alone for God is always with us

CONTRASTING COLORS 

How does this compare to the anointing of the Christian believer?

• • • • • • •

"We are to stand out in the world as our anointing affects those around us"

- We are holy and set apart
- Recognizable from a distance
- Not only do we stand out, we do not blend in
- We no longer walk in the dark
- Humility shines the light of God
- God defines our value and shows us His purpose
- Promotion follows those who follow God

EXTREMELY BOLD

What makes the Christian believer bold, courageous, and powerful?

• • • • • • •

"The Whole Armor of God"

- We can be fearless cause greater is He who is living in us than he that is in this world
- God has equipped us for the battles and we must wear the Full Armor because of the spiritual warfare going on around us
- Pray on all occasions and draw strength from the Lord
- Be ready to cast out devils as need be

MASTERFUL FISHERMAN 

What does it mean for the Christian believer to be a masterful fisherman?

• • • • • • •

"Lock-in, swoop down, clean your nets – Commitment, focus and preparation"

- We must have a strong commitment to whatever service God has called us into
- To be good fisher of men we must be focused on God and His calling
- Praying and fasting are powerful ways to prepare and receive direction from God
- Seek the Lord and take time to study and show yourself approved
- Testimonies are one of the most powerful tools in your tacklebox
- Compassion, patience, and love are requirements to be masterful fishers of men

SUMMARY

In summary, we are God's eagles. We live holy, for we choose to live high on the Mount of God, far above the corruption that is in the world. We soar high on the wind of the Holy Spirit. We are kings and priests in the kingdom of God. We show forth His light as we minister before Him with the world watching. We choose to look more with our spiritual eyes than with our natural eyes, for faith sees what God sees.

Through every season, we can rely on God to help us grow. In times of preparation, we know that God is working in us to bring out the best He has in store for our lives. We are faithful to our First

Love, Jesus Christ, who gave Himself for us that we could become the bride of Christ; we will be forever married to our Lord and Savior. Though we will have individual assignments that only we can do, through the power of the Holy Spirit, we are never alone, for God is with us.

With the anointing of the Holy Spirit, we are able to stand out for Christ bringing many into His family. We are exceedingly bold; unafraid of what man or devil can do to us. For we are equipped as more than conquerors through Christ who loves us. Through our focus, commitment, and preparation, we fish for men just as Christ commanded us.

YOU ARE AN EAGLE. GO AND DO AS EAGLES DO...

- Through the power of the Holy Spirit you are able to nest in heavenly heights, you **RIGHTEOUS EAGLE**.
- Fly on with the Holy Spirit, you **SOARING EAGLE.**
- Rule over your territory - you **MAJESTIC EAGLE**.
- See with your spiritual eyes - you **VIGILANT EAGLE**.
- You will fly high above the storm, you patient, **HIGH-FLYING EAGLE**.

- Remain joyful, for you are being groomed into a victorious flier, you **CONQUERING EAGLE**.
- Journey on, you **FAITHFUL EAGLE**.
- Fly solo, you **MIGHTY EAGLE**.
- Fly so you can be seen, you **BEAUTIFUL AND RADIANT EAGLE**.
- Fly boldly, you **POWERFUL EAGLE**.
- With the help of the Holy Spirit you are well-able to reel in a harvest for Jesus, you **MASTERFUL EAGLE**.

PRAYER

Father God, in the mighty name of Jesus, we give You thanks. Thank You for teaching us about the magnificent eagle and how it relates to us. May we never forget that we are Yours. Remind us that we are able, through the power of the Holy Spirit, to soar in victory over any situation that comes our way. May we remember the words that You spoke to us through this book. We are Your eagles.

Jesus, help us to live holy. Help us rely on You more and more each day. Show us what You see. Father, show us the seasons and timings of the Spirit. Guard us with Your peace and help us to remain patient in trial and tribulation. In times of wilderness, show us that You are working it out for Your glory and our benefit. Build us up as holy temples that can stand out with the anointing of the Holy Spirit to do what You have called us to do. Make us bold. Help us fish well. Point out to us those we need to set a net for. We will be careful to give You the glory and the honor that is due unto Your name.

We cannot do this without Your help. We are dedicated to You. To do Your will, oh God, is our greatest desire. It is our privilege to be eagles in Your name. We give You all the praise, honor, and glory. We thank You for doing it. In the precious name of Jesus I pray. Amen.

ABOUT THE AUTHOR

Spread Your Wings and Soar

I grew up in Indianapolis, Indiana, in a Christian home. My dad was the Late Deacon George D. Williams, Sr., and my mother was the Late Sister Emma Williams. Both received Christ before I was born. I received Christ in my life in 1969 as a child. I have been blessed to have walked with the Lord all my life. I was married (1974) to my childhood sweetheart, Lady Sarion J. Williams. We had 4 children (2 girls and 2 boys), but we lost our oldest son when he was 20-years old due to a drive-by shooting. We have 10 grandchildren and 2 great-grandchildren that are all doing well.

I served at my home church, Christ Temple Indianapolis, IN, until relocating to help build a church with Pastor John Rolle in Brazil, IN, in 1976. I have been in church ministry since 1977. In 1980, we relocated to Indy, under Pastor E.Z. Sanders, Sr., and was ordained in 1986 in the Churches of Our Lord Jesus Christ, Inc. I received my first ministry degree from Aenon Bible College in 1985. In 1988, we began pastoral ministry at Full Gospel Worship Center in Indianapolis, IN under the blessings of District Elder Alonzo Moyer.

In 2015, we connected with the World Fellowship of Independent Ministries with Bishop J. Lavern Tyson as the overseer. In 2017, I was elevated to the office of a Bishop in WFIM. In 2018, I received my second ministry degree from Indiana Wesleyan

University. In 2020, the leadership of WFIM was turned over to me and I became the Overseer of WFIM. April 17, 2023, marks 35 years in pastoral ministry at what is now called Absolute Worship Ministries. All praise to God for using us to be a blessing to help empower men and women of God in the service of our Lord Jesus Christ!

Soon, I will be in the pastoral ministry for 35 years. God has allowed me during my pastoral ministry to ordain ten gifted ministers of the Gospel. He has used me in the gift of healing many times. God has granted me the opportunity to preach the gospel in many places across the U.S.

I have had the opportunity to travel to several foreign countries (Haiti, Jamaica). I visited these places to do missionary work by helping to build and repair homes and an orphanage. I have plans to visit Africa and other countries in the near future. I am also looking forward to using all that God has given me to be one of His best spiritual eagles.

Special thanks to all of you that have supported this first book project. I truly appreciate you and pray that you have been empowered by what you have read. It was my desire to use this information to help us see the beauty of what God created us to be in Him. If this book has been a blessing to you please feel free to drop me a line at bishopgdwjr@gmail.com.

SPREAD YOUR WINGS AND SOAR

About the Author

If you would like to financially support us as we continue to bless the body of Christ, send to my cashapp: $bishopgdwms2 (scan QR code).

FUTURE PUBLISHING GOALS:

- Voices from the Past
- Preacher's Notes
- Till Death Do We Part (Marriage)
- Church 101
- Historical ministry blog (website)

In the Service of Jesus,
Bishop George Williams, Jr.

SPREAD YOUR WINGS AND SOAR

About the Author

ABOUT THE PUBLISHER

Spread Your Wings and Soar

Logos Man Publishing is committed to sharing the Word of God to empower people to believe in Christ through various media such as print, digital, audio, and video. Visit our website at logosmanpublishing.com to support our mission and browse our resources.

Logos Man Publishing

SPREAD YOUR WINGS AND SOAR

About the Publisher